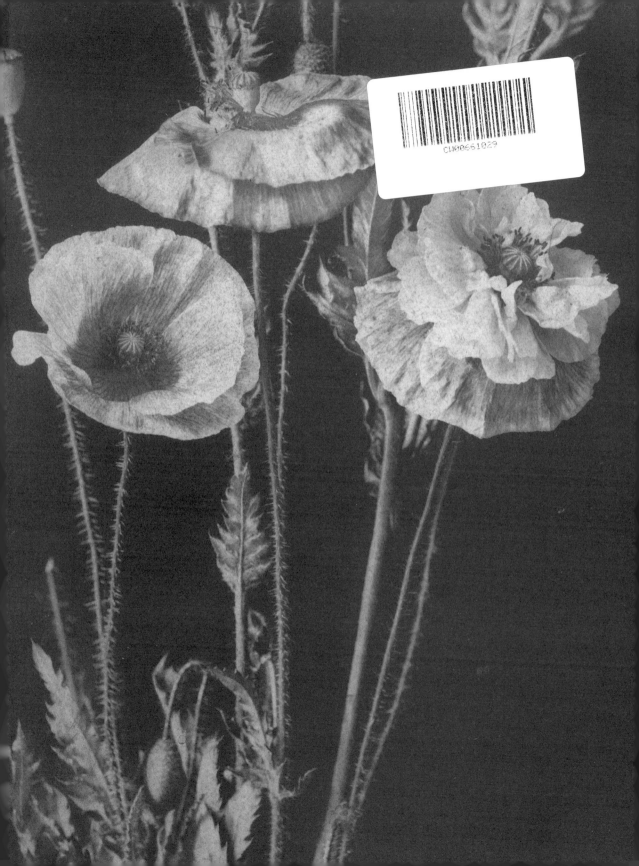

THE LAMPS *of* TIFFANY STUDIOS
Nature Illuminated

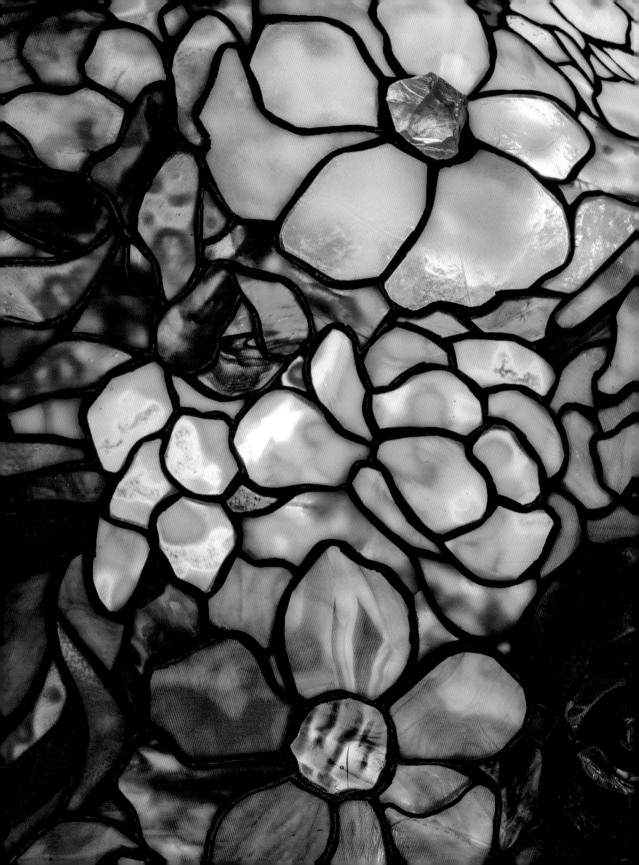

THE LAMPS *of* TIFFANY STUDIOS

Nature Illuminated

THE NEUSTADT COLLECTION AT THE

NEW-YORK HISTORICAL SOCIETY

MARGARET K. HOFER *with* REBECCA KLASSEN

Photography by COLIN COOKE

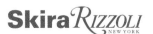

NEW-YORK HISTORICAL SOCIETY
MUSEUM & LIBRARY

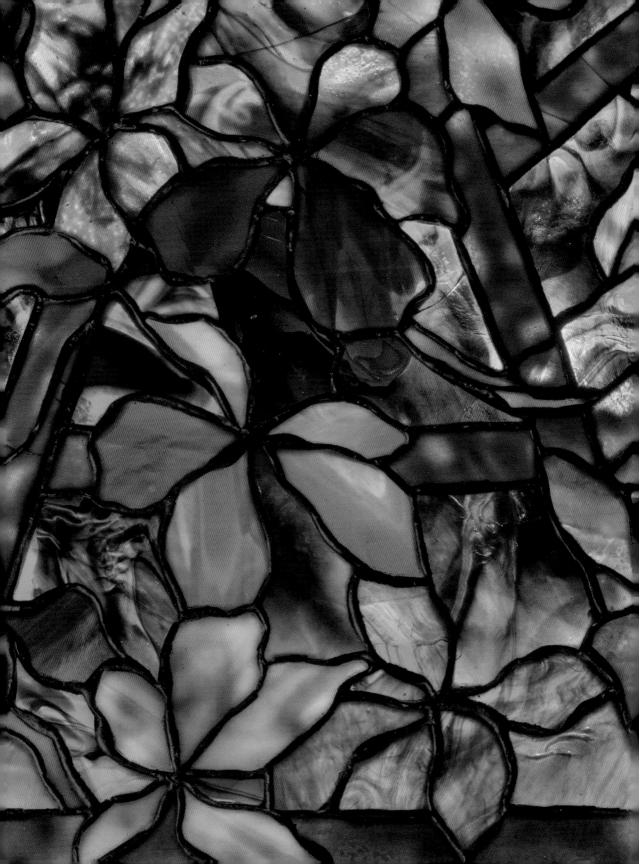

FOREWORD

ONE OF THE GREATEST TREASURES OF THE NEW-YORK Historical Society Museum is its collection of Tiffany Studios lamps, donated by the visionary collector Dr. Egon Neustadt in 1983. Recognized as one of the largest and most encyclopedic collections of Tiffany lamps in the world, the trove provides compelling evidence of the artistic genius of Louis C. Tiffany and his talented designers and artisans. It is also, of course, a visual feast of nature's splendor.

In 2007, guest curators Martin Eidelberg and the late Nina Gray, along with my colleague, New-York Historical Society Museum Director Margaret K. Hofer, organized the groundbreaking exhibition *A New Light on Tiffany: Clara Driscoll and the Tiffany Girls*. The exhibition revealed, for the very first time, the critical role that women played in the design and manufacture of Tiffany Studios lamps and other luxury goods. Eidelberg, Gray, and Hofer deployed the Neustadt Collection as the nucleus of the exhibition, identifying lamps once presumed to be the work of Tiffany as the designs of Clara Driscoll, head of Tiffany's Women's Glass Cutting Department, with glass artistically selected by Driscoll's team of "Tiffany Girls."

The Lamps of Tiffany Studios: Nature Illuminated, featuring eighty representative examples from the Neustadt Collection, is published in conjunction with the unveiling of a dazzling new Tiffany lamp gallery on New-York Historical's renovated fourth floor. This book and the gallery foreground the story of the women who labored in anonymity to create some of these masterpieces. Recently conserved and newly photographed by Colin Cooke, the lamps sparkle as they did when they left the workshops of Tiffany Studios more than a century ago.

I am enormously grateful to Margaret K. Hofer for her collegiality and her knowledge and talent, without which this ambitious new gallery and its companion publication would not have been possible. I am also grateful to New-

York Historical's Board of Trustees, led by Chair Pam B. Schafler, Executive Committee Chair Roger Hertog, and Vice Chair Richard Reiss, Jr. The Board's enlightened support for this and other projects goes to the heart of our institution's success.

Louise Mirrer, PhD
President and CEO
New-York Historical Society

ACKNOWLEDGMENTS

WITH THIS PUBLICATION, WE CELEBRATE the rejuvenation of the New-York Historical Society's Neustadt Collection, soon to be installed in a new, multilevel gallery dedicated to Tiffany lamps. The lamps' physical renewal was overseen by expert stained glass conservator Thomas Venturella, who joined forces with conservator Jim Murphy, electrician Lenny Lapadula, and metalworker Jeremy Lebensohn. Susan Tomlin and Mary Clerkin Higgins undertook skillful shade conservation, while Paul Crist and Joe Jewel brought invaluable expertise to lamp hardware. For her indispensable advice throughout the project, I am deeply grateful to Arlie Sulka of Lillian Nassau LLC. Photographer Colin Cooke and digital retoucher Michael Marquand, with the aid of art handler Peter Schenck, brought the lamps to life in stunning photographs created expressly for this book. The essay and chronology are indebted to the work of Martin Eidelberg, the late Nina Gray, and Alice Cooney Frelinghuysen, whose writings have greatly expanded scholarship on Tiffany Studios. Last but far from least, I thank editor Anne Hoy for her incisive comments and my collaborator Rebecca Klassen for steering conservation and photography, as well as bringing fresh perspective to these beloved objects.

Margaret K. Hofer
Vice President and Museum Director
New-York Historical Society

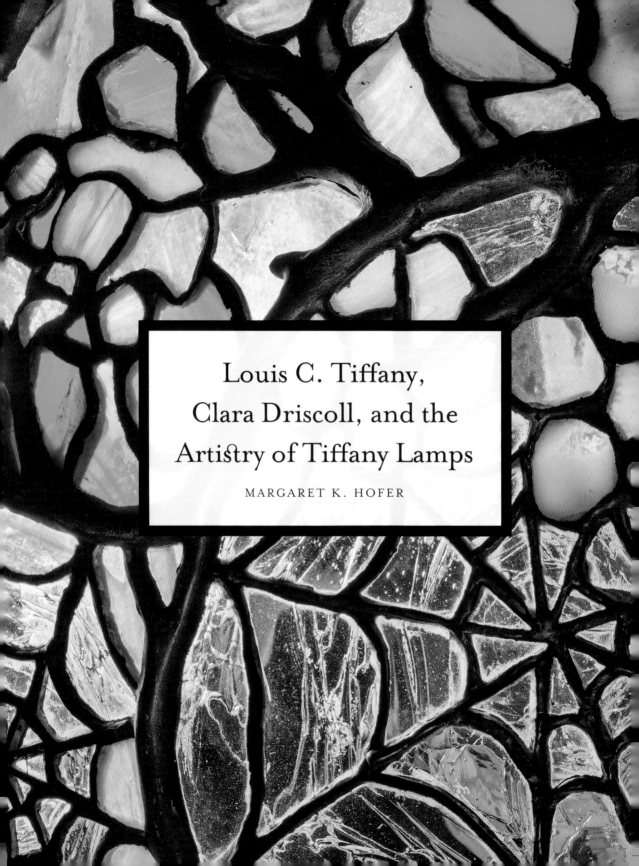

Louis C. Tiffany, Clara Driscoll, and the Artistry of Tiffany Lamps

MARGARET K. HOFER

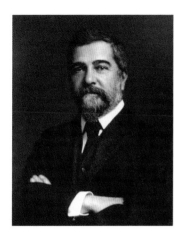

THE JEWEL-LIKE LAMPS MADE BY TIFFANY STUDIOS under the direction of Louis C. Tiffany are icons of early twentieth-century American design. Indeed, "Tiffany lamp" has become a generic term for a vast array of leaded glass shades, from the lamps by Tiffany's competitors to the handiwork of hobbyists to the pale imitations that sprouted in fern bars across the country from the late 1960s through the 1980s. Tiffany's leaded glass lamps incorporated the then-recent innovation of incandescent light bulbs, softening their intensity with shades of shimmering glass that poetically rendered the natural world. These sumptuous lamps were products of the Gilded Age, a period of prosperity that persisted until the arrival of World War I. They reflect the genius of one of the era's most celebrated artists, as well as the prodigious talent of designers who worked in anonymity to fulfill his aesthetic vision. Together, they married art and industry to bring the beauty of nature into the American home.

Tiffany Studios was one of a succession of firms that flourished under the direction of Louis C. Tiffany (1848–1933; fig. 1), son of the internationally renowned jewelry and silver retailer Charles L. Tiffany (1812–1902). The younger Tiffany, opting to pursue art rather than join his father's firm, trained as a landscape painter, but by the early 1880s shifted his focus to interior design. He strove to integrate the visual arts, creating harmonious environments that melded elements of East and West and that, above all, took inspiration from nature. Tiffany summed up his approach: "Every really great structure is simple in its lines—as in Nature,—every great scheme of decoration thrusts no one note upon the eye. No plan of lighting makes its source predominant, and the charm of homes of refinement is in the artistic blending that is revealed when everything has its place and purpose, and when every detail unites to form one perfect and complete whole."[1]

Tiffany was captivated by the creative possibilities of glass and pushed the boundaries of the art form. Along with his competitor John La Farge (1835–1910), he pioneered the manufacture of opalescent glass, a milky, multicolored glass that could be made in an extraordinary range of hues and manipulated while molten to achieve three-dimensional effects. The use of opalescent glass revolutionized the stained glass window industry: artisans no longer achieved most details by painting *on* glass, as stained glass artisans had done for centuries—they painted *with* glass. By the 1890s, Tiffany's firm had become the country's leading manufacturer of leaded glass windows and had achieved national and international recognition for its innovative blown glass, marketed under the trade name "Favrile."

An outgrowth of Tiffany Studios' work in windows, the firm's leaded glass lamps did not appear until around 1898, more than two decades after Tiffany's initial experiments in glassmaking. His early lamps, typically featuring blown glass shades or bases, are heavily proportioned, densely ornamented creations that evoke Middle Eastern and South Asian aesthetics. The design of these experimental lighting devices, the majority fueled by kerosene, was constrained by the need to conceal a reservoir in the base. Although Thomas Edison patented his incandescent light bulb in 1880, paving the way for a new era of lighting, electricity was not widespread in New York City homes until the second decade of the twentieth century. The light bulb liberated Tiffany's lamp designs: his electric bases, which he began producing by 1898, did not require the heavy bulbousness needed for fuel models and have lighter, more elegant profiles.

It has often been presumed that the lamps, windows, and other luxury objects produced by Tiffany Studios were designed exclusively by Tiffany himself. While he was undeniably the firm's guiding force, recent scholarship has

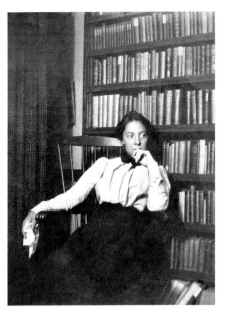

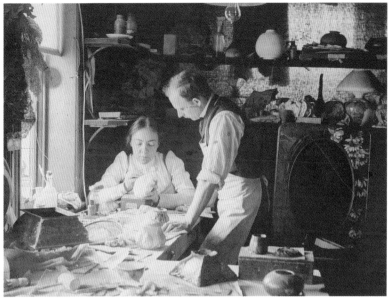

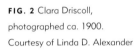

FIG. 2 Clara Driscoll, photographed ca. 1900. Courtesy of Linda D. Alexander

FIG. 3 Clara Driscoll in her workroom at Tiffany Studios with her chief assistant Joseph Briggs, 1901. Department of American Decorative Arts, Metropolitan Museum of Art, New York

revealed the substantial contributions of the women (and men) who labored behind the scenes, uncredited, to create the masterpieces now inextricably linked to the Tiffany name. The critical role of designer Clara Driscoll, née Wolcott (1861–1944; figs. 2, 3), was brought to the fore through caches of her correspondence discovered by historians in 2005. As head of the Women's Glass Cutting Department at Tiffany Studios, Driscoll designed the vast majority of Tiffany lampshades with nature-based themes—including many of the firm's iconic lampshades—and numerous other objects. In fact, the very idea of creating leaded glass shades may have largely been hers.[2] Her letters also bring to light the instrumental role of the employees she called "Tiffany Girls"—the women who worked under her supervision, selecting and cutting glass for lampshades, windows, and mosaics.[3]

Born in Tallmadge, Ohio, Clara Pierce Wolcott moved to New York City to complete her art training and find work in the burgeoning field of industrial arts. She was hired by Tiffany in June 1888, but left the firm the next year when she married Francis S. Driscoll. Following her husband's untimely death in 1892, she returned to head the newly formed Women's Glass Cutting Department, which eventually

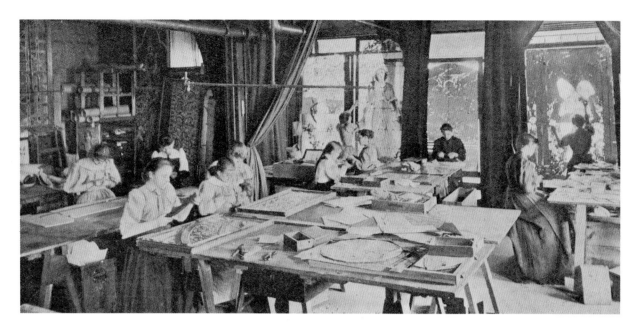

employed some thirty-five women (fig. 4). During her early years at Tiffany, Driscoll worked on the firm's mosaics and leaded glass windows, which laid the groundwork for her early lamp designs.

Driscoll's letters describe the productive collaboration she enjoyed with "Mr. Tiffany," who met with her regularly to critique her ideas. Their relationship was fueled by a shared artistic vision, including a love of nature and an appreciation of beautiful materials. Her designs took full advantage of the innovations in color and texture pioneered by Tiffany's glassmakers. Although she generally worked independently, Driscoll's aesthetic sense blossomed under Tiffany's direction. Her earliest lamps are extravagant and sculptural. The *Butterfly*, inspired by a memory of butterflies swarming above a field of primrose blossoms in her Ohio hometown, features a leaded shade swathed in swirling metalwork and a mosaic-encrusted base set in a rich bronze framework.[4] The *Cobweb* (pl. 51), with a similarly sculptural mosaic base depicting narcissus, bears the hallmarks of Driscoll's design sensibility and was probably conceived shortly after the *Butterfly*. In 1899, she hit upon the idea of a *Dragonfly* lamp, which hatched numerous variations and became one of the firm's most popular and enduring lamp designs (pls. 19–23).[5] Tiffany was so enamored of her design—which depicted the iridescent insects with filigree wings and inset glass eyes—that he had the women's department rush the production of several examples, one displayed at the Grafton Galleries in London and another exhibited at the Paris World's Fair of 1900.[6] At the exposition, Driscoll's lyrical design won a bronze medal and earned her a rare instance of public recognition.[7]

By 1900, Tiffany had expanded his empire by increasing the firm's production of *objets de luxe*: not only an array of lamps for fuel and electricity, but a lavish assortment of "fancy goods," including inkstands, candlesticks, clocks, small boxes, tea screens, and other decorative but functional objects. The bronze foundry established at his Corona, Queens, plant in 1897 enabled enlarged and more diversified production, particularly a profusion of cast bronze and spun metal lamp bases. By the time Tiffany Studios released its *Price List* of October 1, 1906, the firm boasted hundreds of models in production, ranging in price from $30 to a princely $750.[8] An important feature of the firm's lamp stock was the interchangeability of components: with most models, customers could mix or match bases and shades to suit their tastes and harmonize with virtually any domestic interior.

Driscoll's talent and prolific output, coupled with the artistic selection of glass executed by the Tiffany Girls, helped propel the success of Tiffany's lamp business. Around 1901, she designed the *Wisteria*, an electric model topped with branchlike bronze openwork and featuring a mass of cascading blossoms. The shade is supported on a sculptural bronze base, twisted like a gnarled tree trunk (pls. 43, 44). The fabulously popular *Wisteria* retailed for $400 in 1906, making it one of the firm's more expensive models. The base supports similar shades, likely of Driscoll's design, such as

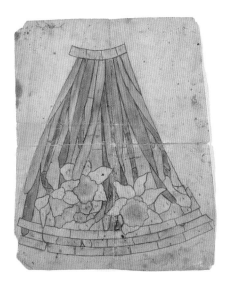

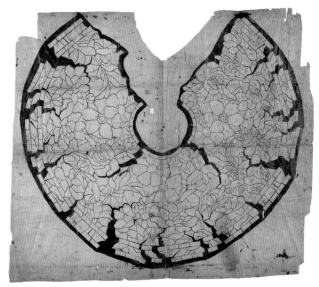

the *Apple Blossom* as well as the *Grape* and the pendulous *Trumpet Creeper* (pls. 47, 48, 68, 74). Ceding, however, to long-term pressure from the firm's business managers, she adopted a more resourceful design method by 1904 based on simpler, more economical cone- or dome-shaped shades.[9]

Surviving design drawings, wooden forms, brass templates, and other tools, as well as Driscoll's remarks in her correspondence, elucidate the process used to make Tiffany lampshades. Tiffany's designers often started with direct observation of nature and relied heavily on photographs of botanical specimens, as demonstrated by the large numbers of floral photographs that survive with the firm's stamp.[10] The designer first created a watercolor sketch showing at least one repeat of the shade's pattern (fig. 5), which was submitted to the factory so that a scale mold could be made in white plaster. Next, the designer outlined the design on the mold and filled it in with watercolor for Tiffany's approval. A mold could accommodate drawn repeats for more than one shade model; for instance, in 1904, Driscoll described creating an *Arrowhead*, a *Daffodil*, and a *Geranium* shade using a single fourteen-inch mold.[11] Approved designs were rendered

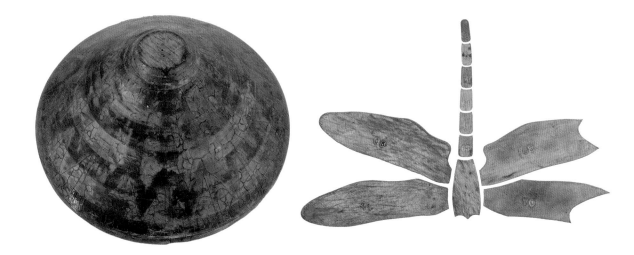

FIG. 7 Wooden block for 20-in. *Arrowhead* shade, ca. 1904, 11 × 20 in. (27.9 × 50.8 cm). New-York Historical Society, Gift of Fred and Nancylee Dikeman

FIG. 8 Patterns for 22-in. *Dragonfly* shade, ca. 1900–06, sheet brass. New-York Historical Society, Gift of Fred and Nancylee Dikeman

as cartoons, or full-size flat drawings (fig. 6), which were transferred to shaped wooden blocks by carefully incising the pattern into the wood (fig. 7). Brass templates cut for each segment of glass guided the glass cutters (fig. 8). In addition, the cartoon was traced in black paint on a flat, framed piece of clear glass known as an easel, which could be held up to the studio window to allow viewing of the selected glass in natural transmitted light. As each piece of glass was selected from the sheets, the glass cutter cut it, coated its edges with beeswax and then thin copper foil, and finally stuck it to the easel with more beeswax. When complete, the entire easel was sent to the men's department, where the segments were soldered together, starting with a metal ring at the top (fig. 9). Finally, the leading was electroplated with copper and given a rich bronze patina to harmonize with the base. For an additional charge, customers could select a more extravagant silver or gold finish.

A single shade design sometimes yielded hundreds of completed examples, particularly in the case of the most popular models. However, each Tiffany lamp is a unique work of art, distinguished by the selection of its glass. Tiffany's selectors—largely women working under Driscoll's

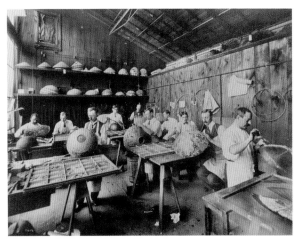

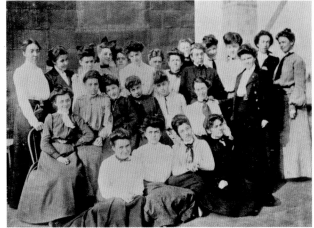

FIG. 9 Workmen in the Lamp
Department assembling shades, ca.
1909–10. Courtesy of the Ellman Family

FIG. 10 Tiffany Girls on the roof of
Tiffany Studios, ca. 1904–05. From
left to right, back row, standing:
Clara Driscoll, Mary Voorhis Schofield
Williams, Marion Losey, Edith Pearsall,
Emma Stanley, Annie Tierney, Annie
Boax, Carrie McNicholl, Edna Book,
Ella Egbert Van Derlip, Nellie Warner,
Alice Wilson, Roberta Hodgins,
Agnes Northrop; middle row: Minnie
Henderson, Marion Palmié, May Tatnell,
Irene Talashea, Julia Zevesky, Anna
Arnoth, Anna Ring; front row, seated:
Mary McVickar, Miss Phillips, Virginia
Demarest, Beatrix Hawthorne. The
Charles Hosmer Morse Museum of
American Art, Winter Park, FL

direction—had ultimate control over a lamp's aesthetic success. The selectors had at their disposal vast stores of richly colored and variously textured sheet glass primarily produced at the Corona factory.[12] Louis C. Tiffany, guided by the belief that women had a superior sense of color and naturalistic design, entrusted most of the nature-themed shades to the Women's Glass Cutting Department. Glass selectors worked in teams with glass cutters, whose work was carefully monitored and recorded, down to the tally of pieces cut per day, as well as the number of pieces broken. Cutters, if they excelled, could rise to become glass selectors and receive a pay increase. Tiffany greatly valued the work of his female employees and paid them on the same scale as the men. Clara Driscoll earned $35 a week ($1,820 per year or approximately $45,000 per year in today's dollars), while glass cutters started at $7.50.[13]

A rivalry existed between the firm's female artisans and the unionized male glaziers, and tensions sometimes flared. Louis C. Tiffany, in fact, initially formed the Women's Glass Cutting Department in 1892 in response to a citywide strike by the male-only Lead Glaziers and Glass Cutters Union. In 1903, the men again threatened to strike, this time to prevent the women's department from continuing their work on windows. Ultimately, the company reached an agreement with the union that limited the number of

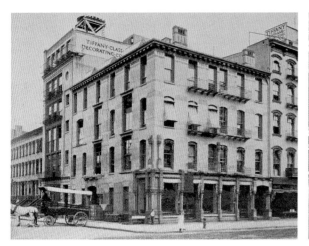

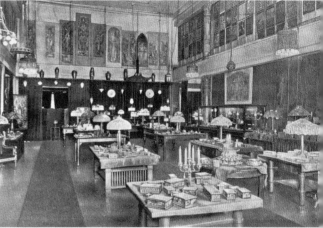

women to twenty-seven, but allowed them to continue their work on windows and lampshades.[14] Despite the men's antagonism, Driscoll managed to secure and even expand her role as a designer, and her department prospered.

Another challenge Driscoll faced was the constant turnover of her workforce. At that time, married women typically did not work if their husbands held a job, and the women at Tiffany's were forced to adhere to this custom. Driscoll herself had left the company upon her first marriage in 1889, only to return three years later after her husband's premature death. The Tiffany Girls (fig. 10), who were as young as fifteen years old, were mostly of marriageable age and rarely stayed employed for long. One exception was Driscoll's colleague Agnes F. Northrop (1857–1953), who joined the women's department in 1894 and went on to become one of Tiffany's most successful window designers.[15]

Tiffany Studios relied on a well-honed business strategy to market its lamps and other deluxe products to the nation's Gilded Age elite. It maintained elaborate showrooms, first at its headquarters on Fourth Avenue (today's Park Avenue South) and Twenty-fifth Street (fig. 11), and after 1905 at a larger and more formal edifice on the corner of Madison Avenue and Forty-fifth Street. A photograph of the Madison Avenue showroom from 1913 shows a banquet of fancy goods amid a sea of leaded glass lamps (fig. 12). The

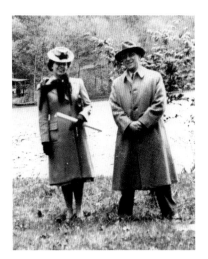

FIG. 13 Egon Neustadt and Hildegard Steininger Neustadt, photographed ca. 1960. The Neustadt Collection of Tiffany Glass, Queens, NY

firm also retailed its products at luxury emporiums around the country, including Marshall Field's in Chicago and J. E. Caldwell in Philadelphia. Regular advertisements and brochures promoted the lamps' artistic merits, distinctive qualities, and wide range of models suited to numerous interiors and budgets.

In 1910, Tiffany Studios published another price list of available products, this one indicating a significant retrenchment in the production of leaded glass shades and fancy goods. Fashion had shifted away from exuberant naturalism to more restrained and historicizing styles. The firm discontinued many models, including the once-popular *Wisteria*, along with the *Trumpet Creeper*, *Apple Blossom*, and *Grape*. Three years later, it issued another price list that signaled further cutbacks in lamp production and a dearth of new designs, save for traditionalist models such as the *Elizabethan* and *Empire* (pls. 10, 11). Whether the two events are related or not, the drastic curtailment of the firm's lamp business coincided with the departure of Clara Driscoll, who left Tiffany Studios by 1909 to marry for a second time, effectively ending her career as a professional artist. A surviving ledger recording the work of the women's department in 1909–10 documents a radically reduced workforce of only five women producing a limited number of shade models.[16] The period of innovation that flourished with the creative partnership of Louis C. Tiffany and Clara Driscoll had come to an end.

An aging Tiffany gradually withdrew from the business after the close of World War I. The men's department continued to fill orders for shades until at least 1924, producing simple geometric models, historicizing styles, and some nature-based shades, such as the *Dragonfly*, *Daffodil*, *Poppy*, and *Peony*.[17] Tiffany Studios filed for bankruptcy in 1932, although unsold stock continued to be offered for several more years. By the time Tiffany died in 1933, his once-daring and original style had long been superseded by the hard-edged, streamlined designs of American Modernism. Tiffany lamps were scorned as passé. As art critic Aline Saarinen declared in 1955, perhaps with some hyperbole, Tiffany products had plummeted from the "peak of chic around 1900 to the gutter of derision around 1920–1930."[18] It took several decades for the art world to reconsider Tiffany's legacy. The first retrospective was held in 1958 at the Museum of Contemporary Crafts (now the Museum of Arts and Design) in New York City, although some collectors had recognized the brilliant achievement of these objects even earlier.

Egon Neustadt (1898–1984), a New York orthodontist, and his wife, Hildegard Steininger (1911–1961), both Austrian immigrants, became pioneer collectors of Tiffany glass at a time when the lamps were still disregarded by most Americans (fig. 13).[19] Shortly after their marriage in 1935, the couple, looking for affordable furnishings for their Queens home, found a "strange, old fashioned" *Daffodil* lamp in a Greenwich Village antique shop and purchased it for $12.50.[20] That modest discovery sparked a decades-long quest in which the Neustadts amassed perhaps the largest and most encyclopedic Tiffany lamp collection in the world: more than two hundred lamps charting the full range of styles produced by the firm. After Hildegard's death, Neustadt continued the pursuit. He published the first major work on the subject, *The Lamps of Tiffany* (1970), in which he attempted to categorize the lamps and provide a framework for understanding the wide range of production. In 1984, Dr. Neustadt donated 132 of his finest lamps to the New-York Historical Society.

The following selection, composed of eighty of the most magnificent examples from the Neustadt donation, offers a visual feast. Photographed especially for this book, the lamps pay homage to some two decades of nature-inspired creativity and innovation at Tiffany Studios. ∎

FOLLOWING PAGES
Detail of lamp 63

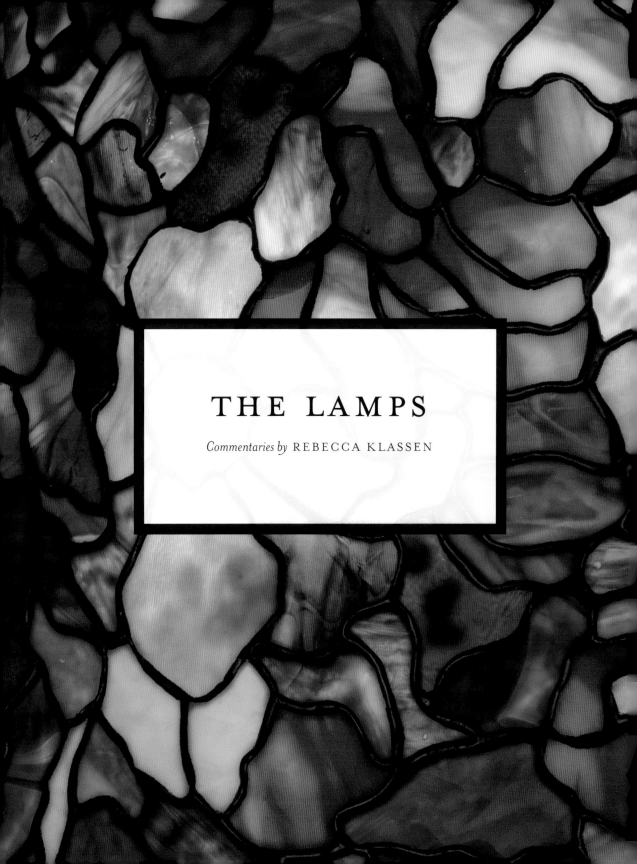

THE LAMPS

Commentaries by REBECCA KLASSEN

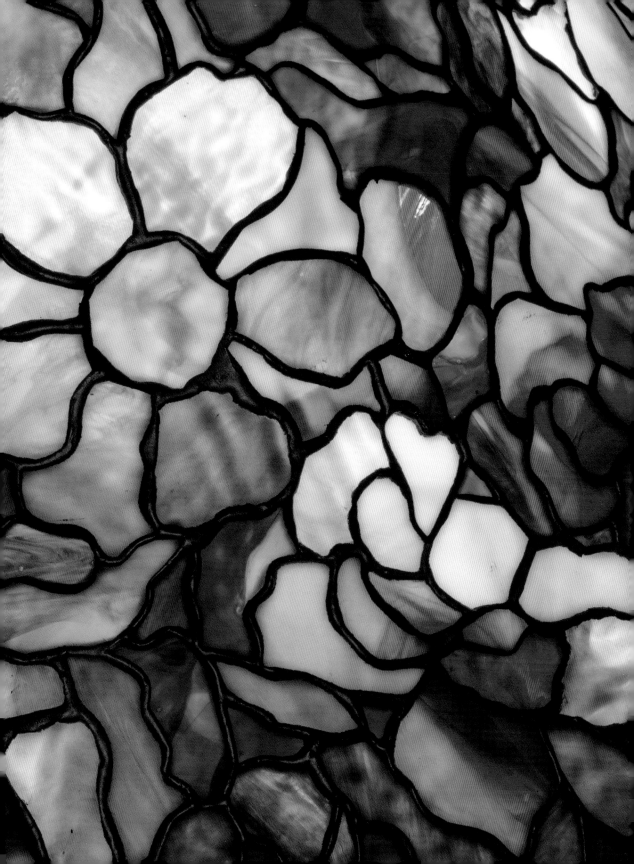

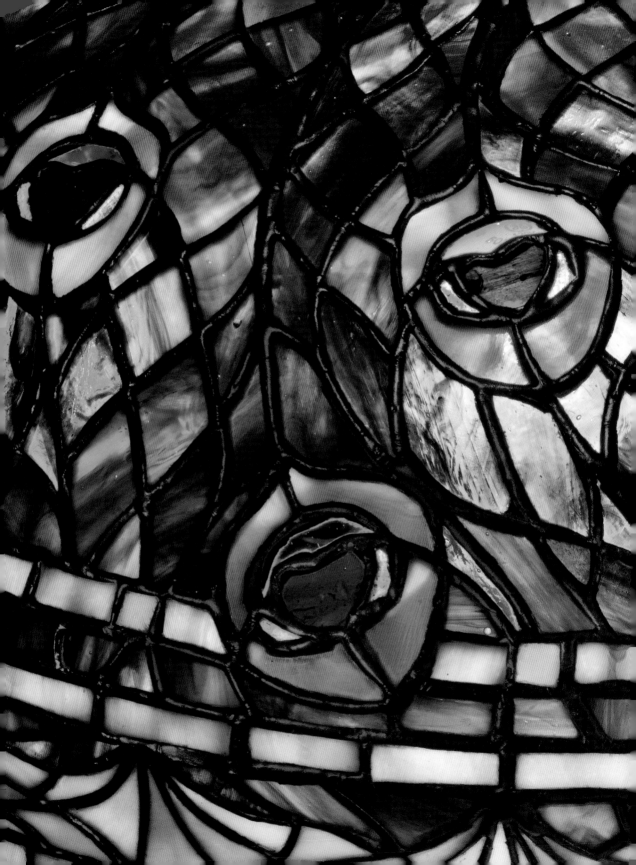

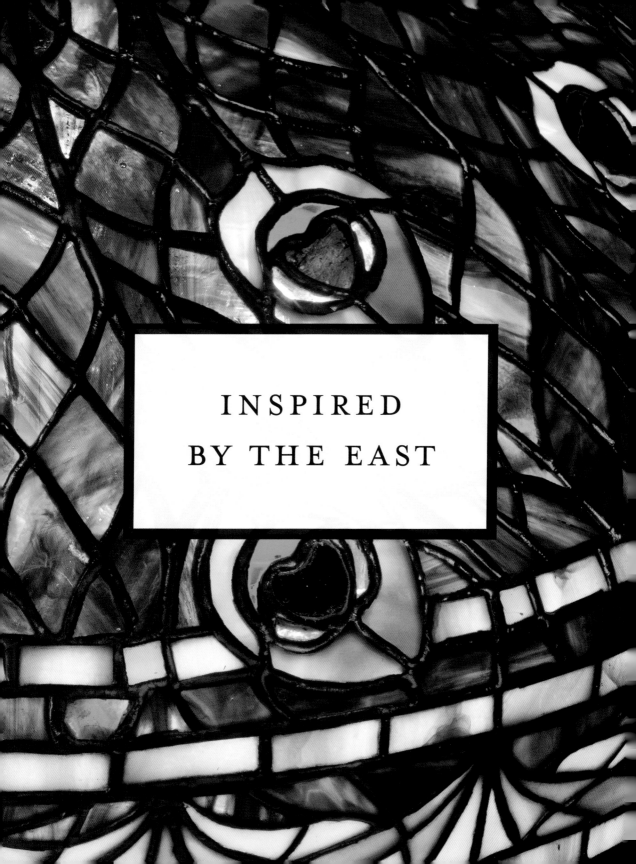

INSPIRED
BY THE EAST

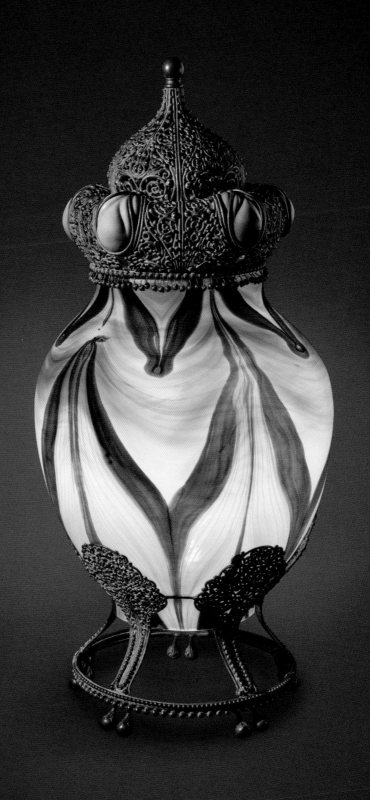

1 *HURRICANE* LAMP
Designed ca. 1894–96

Louis C. Tiffany's travels in North Africa shaped his interests and creative output from 1870 onward. But he initially did not have to look that far for inspiration: Edward C. Moore, head silversmith at Tiffany & Co. from 1851 to 1891, had begun to incorporate East Asian and Islamic aesthetics into his designs around 1867, and would become a major collector of Islamic glass.

Tiffany formed his own wide-ranging collections. His examples of ancient Mediterranean glass were likely the basis for the blown *Hurricane*'s pulled feather decoration, made by dragging a pick through applied colored glass threads while still molten. The intended illumination of the *Hurricane*, with its Persian-inspired filigree crown and stand, remains unclear. Fitted for electric lighting in the mid-twentieth century, it may have originally been used for candlelight.

PRECEDING PAGES
Detail of lamp 8

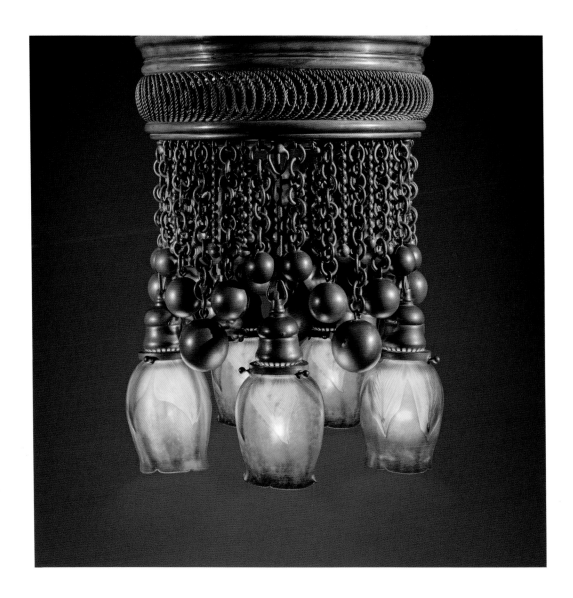

**2 MOORISH CHANDELIER WITH
FAVRILE SHADES**

Designed ca. 1900

3 *STALACTITE* HANGING SHADE

Designed ca. 1904–10

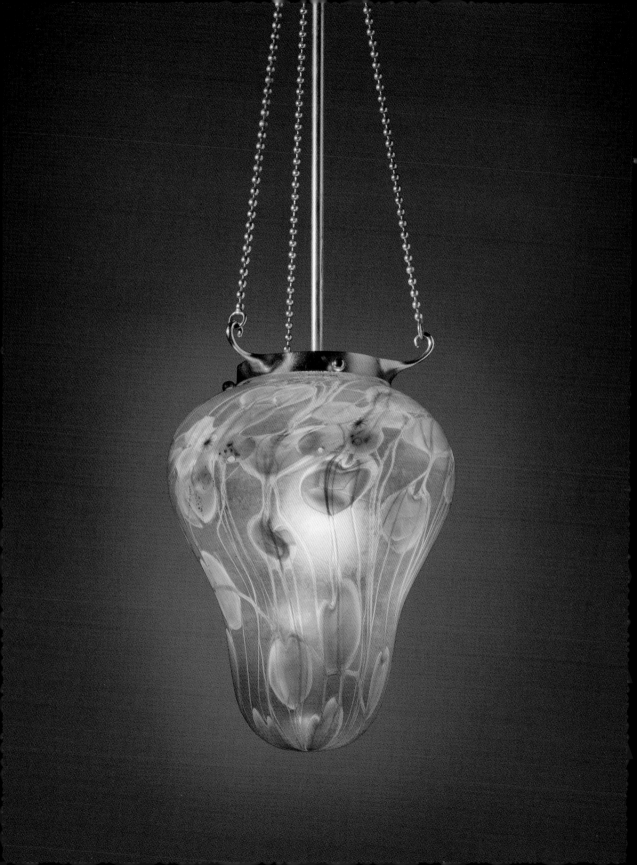

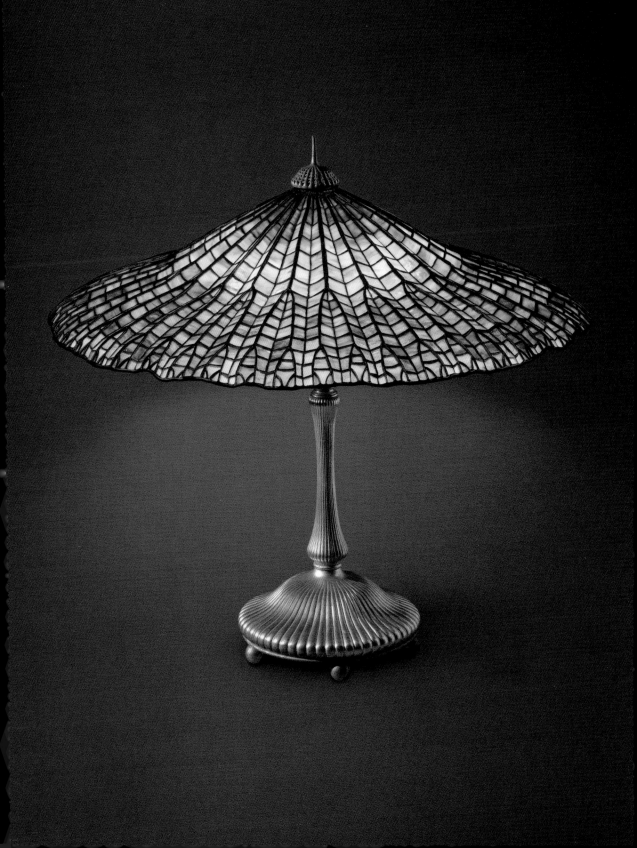

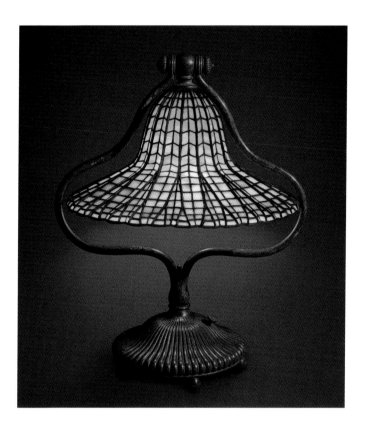

OPPOSITE

4 *LOTUS, PAGODA* SHADE

Designed ca. 1900–04

MUSHROOM BASE

Designed ca. 1900–02

ABOVE

5 *BELL* LAMP AND *LOTUS* SHADE

Designed ca. 1900–06

As named in the Tiffany Studios 1906 *Price List*, "lotus" conjures perfumed fantasies of Eastern mysticism, especially when paired with "pagoda," the tiered sacred building form emblematic of Asia since the seventeenth century. At the same time, the shade's robust geometric scheme resembles the ribbed underside of a giant Victoria water lily pad. The Amazonian plant was widely publicized after English gardeners at Chatsworth succeeded in getting a specimen to flower in 1849. Head gardener Joseph Paxton upheld the pads as marvels of natural engineering, and their structural principles influenced his design for the glass-and-iron Crystal Palace for the 1851 Great Exhibition in London. Through the late nineteenth century, Continental and American conservatories acquired their own showy examples, helping to popularize water lilies for gardening at any scale, from lakes to tubs.

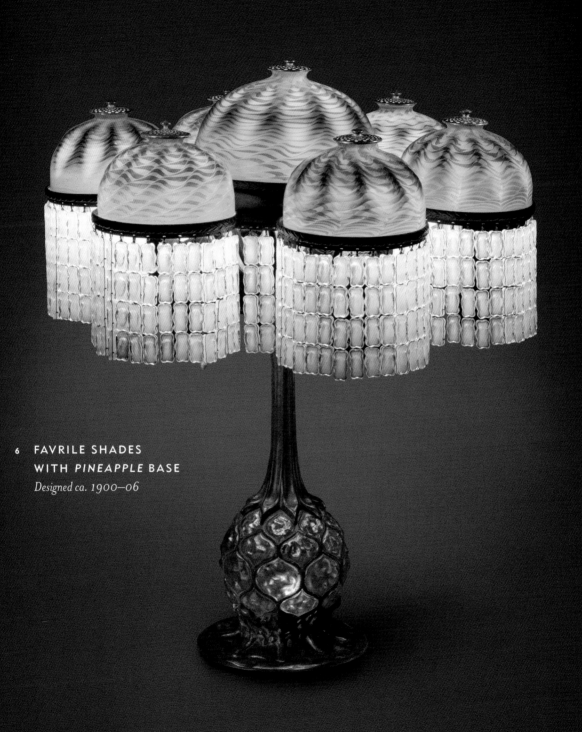

6 **FAVRILE SHADES WITH *PINEAPPLE* BASE**
Designed ca. 1900–06

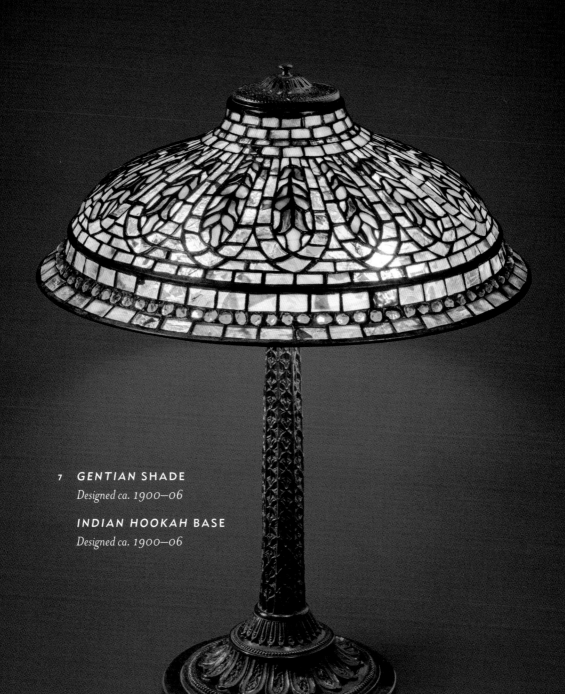

7 **GENTIAN SHADE**
Designed ca. 1900—06

INDIAN HOOKAH BASE
Designed ca. 1900—06

8 *PEACOCK* SHADE
Probably designed by Clara Driscoll ca. 1900–06

PEACOCK BASE
Designed ca. 1900–06

Peacocks—iridescent, glorious—signaled individualism and the pursuit of pure beauty to Aesthetic movement artists and designers from the 1860s through the end of the century, and to Art Nouveau's proponents into the early twentieth century. The birds, native to South and Southeast Asia, were also a Tiffany favorite. Peacocks roamed the grounds of Laurelton Hall, his estate on Long Island, New York, and he held a grandiose Peacock Feast there in 1914. Tiffany Studios translated the bird's train of eye-spotted feathers into a variety of objects, including mosaics, iridescent Favrile glass vases, and leaded glass windows and lampshades, such as the *Peacock*. Designed to conceal an oil canister, the broad-shouldered base mimics the proud contours of the peafowl's chest. Tail feathers spill over the foot, rendered with Art Nouveau–style tendrils and punctuated by glass mosaic eyes.

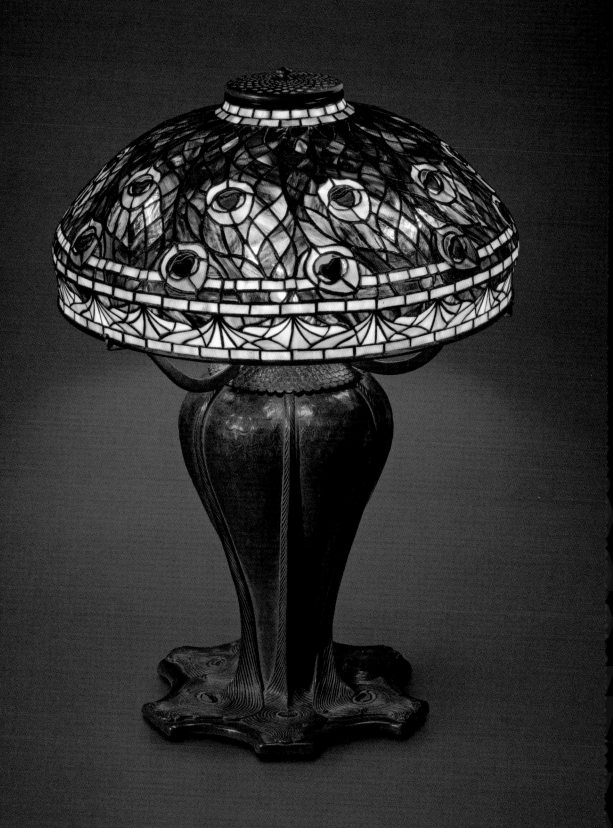

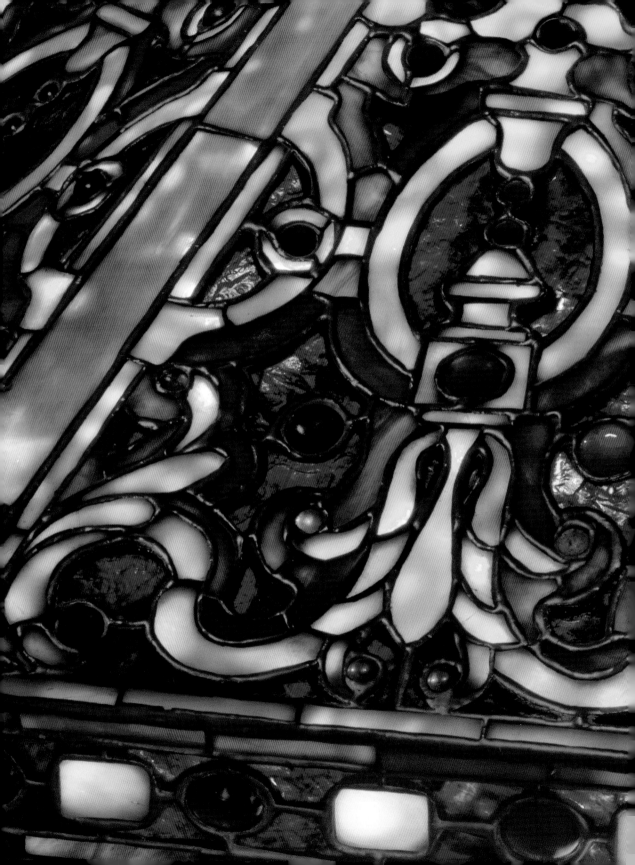

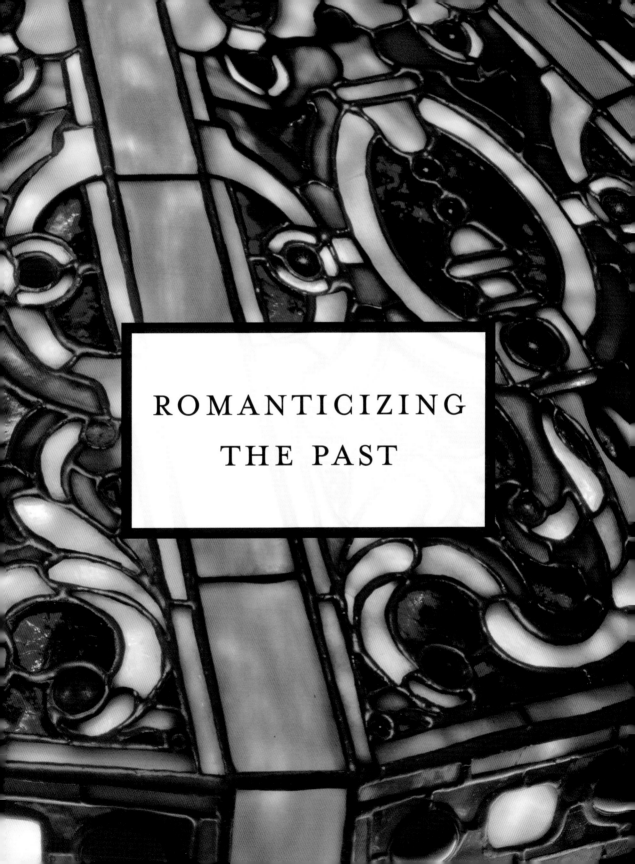

ROMANTICIZING
THE PAST

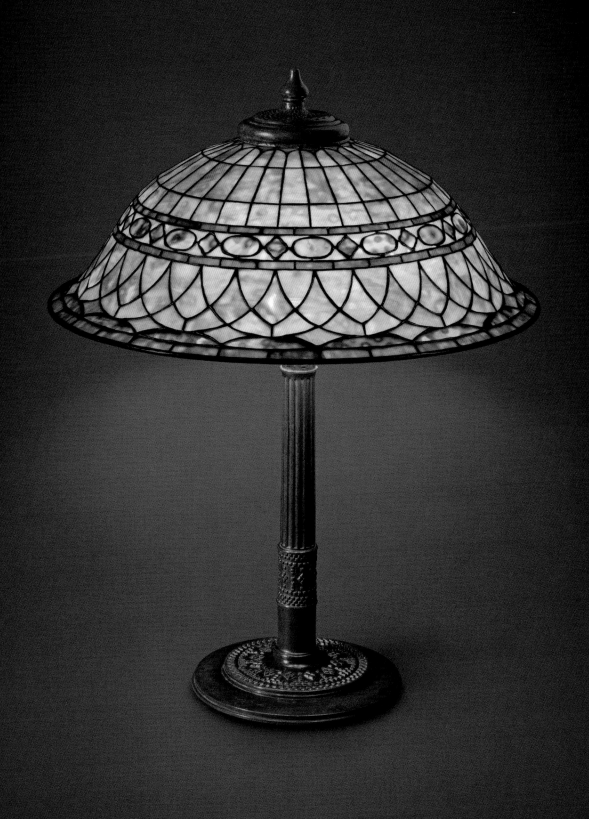

9 *COLONIAL* SHADE

Designed ca. 1906–10

ROMAN BASE

Designed ca. 1906–10

Tiffany decried the imitation of past styles as unimaginative. Yet he was eclectic in his influences, and traditionalism and the startlingly avant-garde coexisted in his interior designs. Advertising itself as a comprehensive decorating resource, Tiffany Studios sold antique and reproduction European and Colonial American objects to suit the tastes of America's wealthy, and its designers produced complementary objects. Promoters of the Colonial Revival style, which flourished from around 1880 to 1930, called on Americans to draw upon their national heritage—often a neoclassical one. The apron design of the *Colonial* shade recalls the tracery patterns in the arches of Palladian windows, a common feature of Colonial Revival homes.

PRECEDING PAGES
Detail of lamp 10

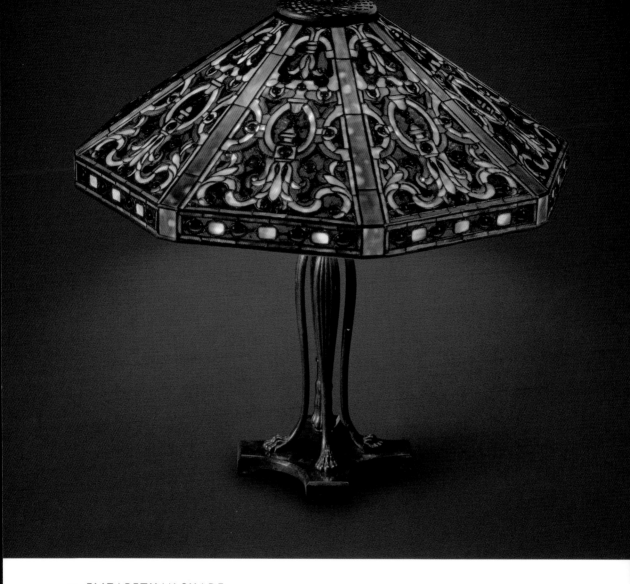

10 *ELIZABETHAN* SHADE

Designed ca. 1910–13

CLAW FEET LIBRARY BASE

Designed ca. 1900–06

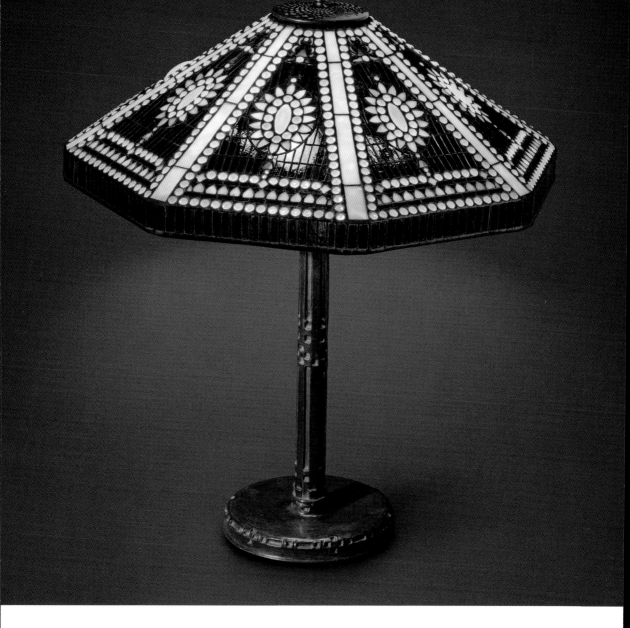

11 *EMPIRE* SHADE

Designed ca. 1910–13

FIFTEENTH CENTURY BASE

Designed ca. 1906–10

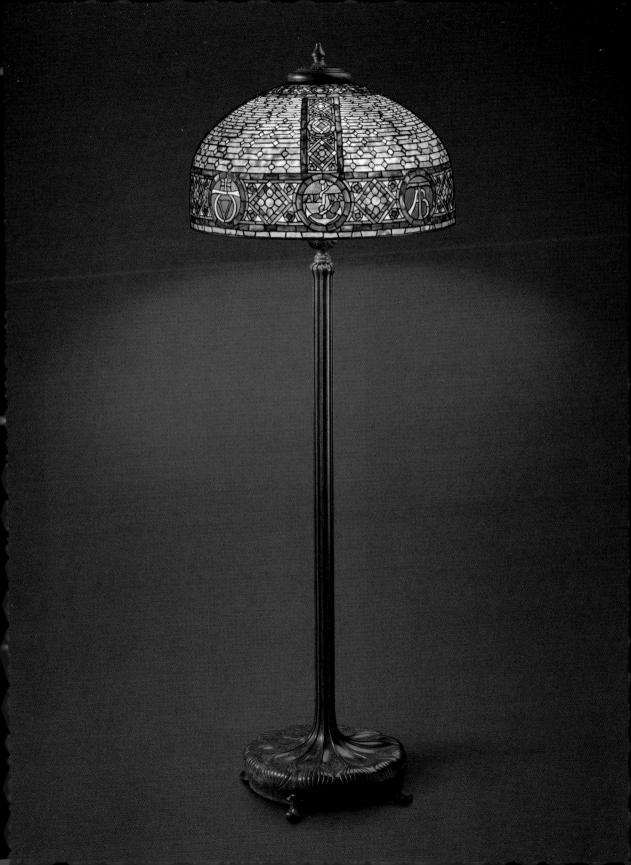

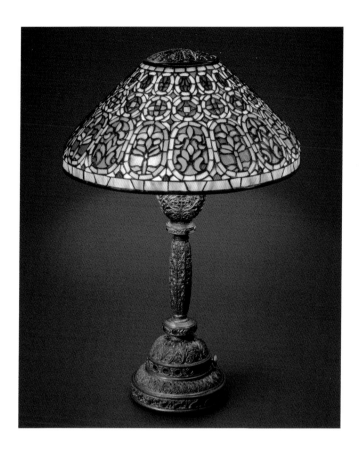

OPPOSITE

12 *BOOKMARK* SHADE

Designed ca. 1906–10

ABOVE

13 *VENETIAN* DESK LAMP

Designed ca. 1906–08

CHASED POD FLOOR BASE

Designed ca. 1900–06

The Arts and Crafts movement's self-conscious retrospection paved the way for the revival of fine printing and bookbinding during the late nineteenth century. Tiffany's own library held volumes describing historic fine book collections. Though not documented in any price list, the floor lamp shade is undoubtedly related to the *Bookmark* metal desk set pattern that Tiffany Studios began producing by 1906. Both pay homage to fifteenth- and sixteenth-century printers through roundels depicting their marks, which they included on title pages and in colophons as a form of authentication. Perhaps the most famous mark—an anchor and dolphin—belongs to Aldus Manutius. His Aldine Press in Venice invented italic type, developed the precursor to the modern pocket book, and first set the semicolon.

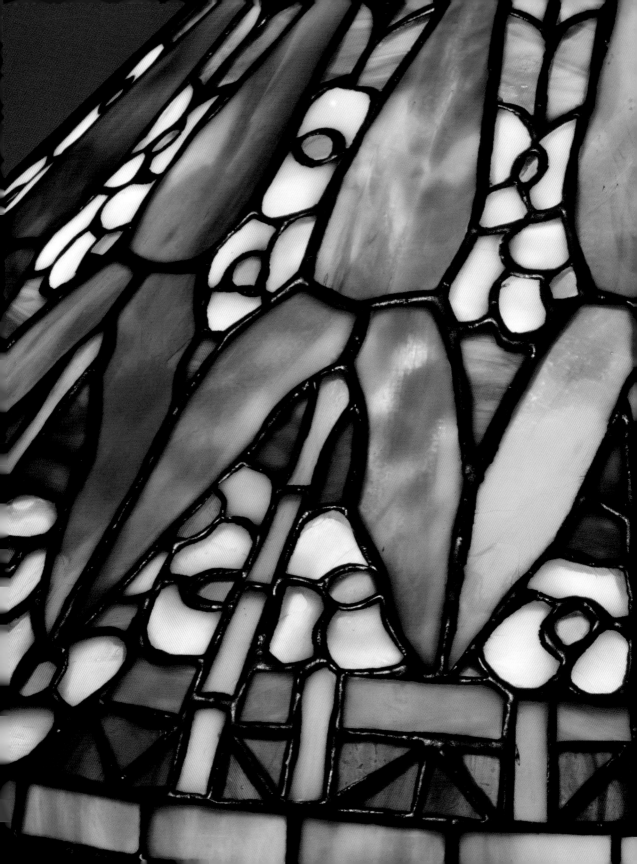

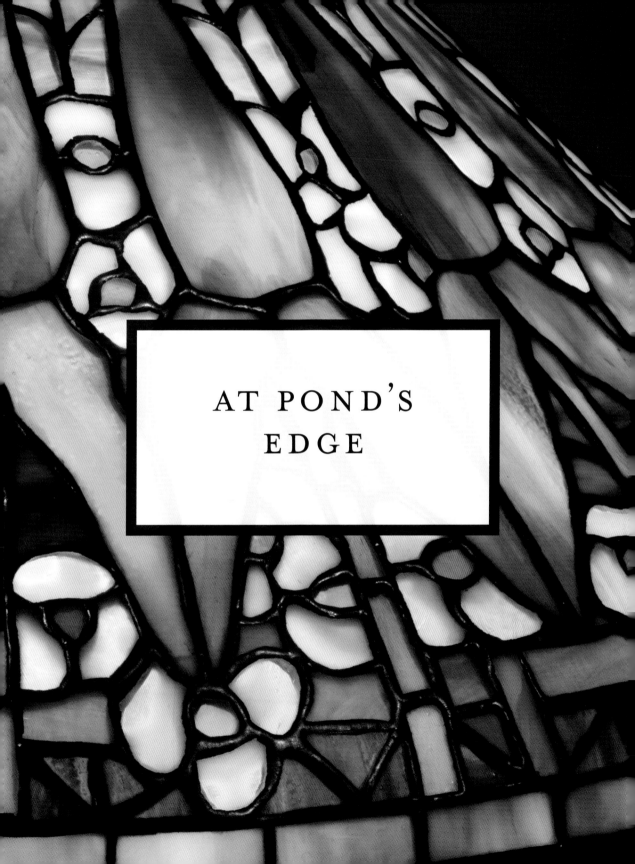

AT POND'S
EDGE

14 *POND LILY* SHADE

Possibly designed by Clara Driscoll ca. 1900—06

BLOWN GLASS IN METAL BASE

Designed ca. 1898—1900

Water lilies first seized the public imagination in the mid-nineteenth century with the spectacles of giant Victoria lilies growing in European and American conservatories, documented by the press and in botanical books. Aquatic gardens began to take hold in the United States in the 1880s and 1890s, when water lilies were placed in public displays and became commercially available. Louis C. Tiffany's Laurelton Hall, built from 1903 to 1905, featured a water lily—filled pond.

The rising interest in aquaculture dovetailed with Japanism in the arts. The leaves of *Pond Lily* overlap around the shade against a clear ground with subtly undulating lead lines, in a pattern resembling the running water motif often found in Japanese cut stencils, or *katagami*, used to create resist-dyed *katazome* fabrics. Tiffany collected these stencils, among other Asian objects.

PRECEDING PAGES
Detail of lamp 16

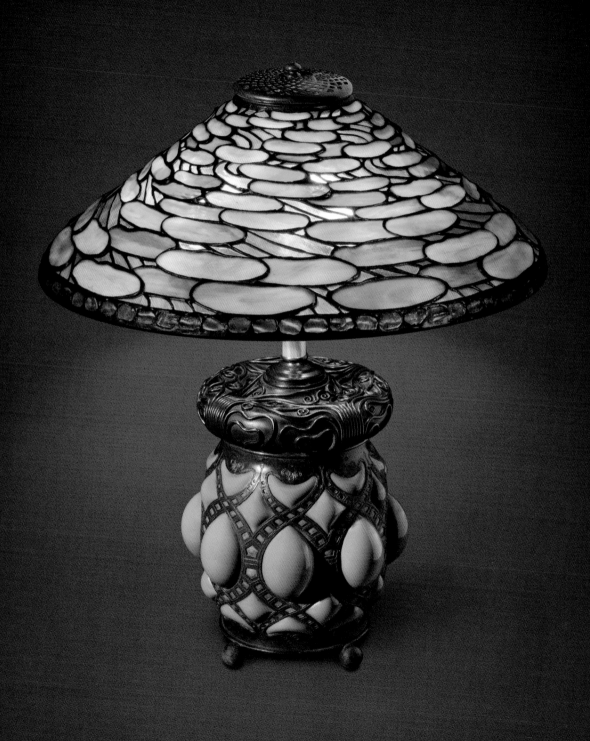

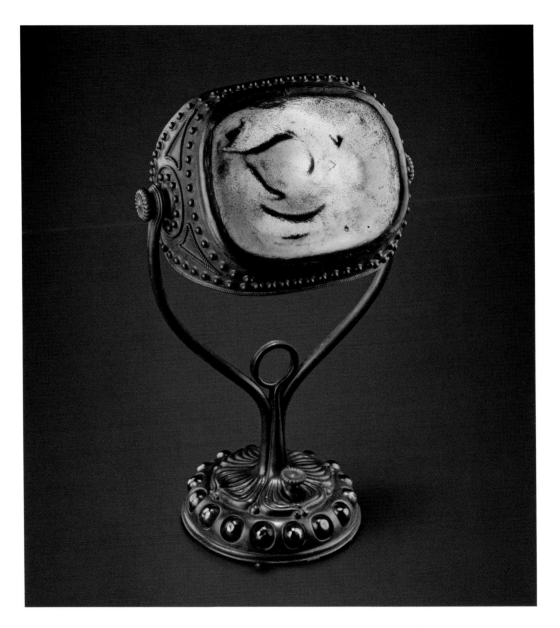

ABOVE

15 *SEAL* LAMP WITH
TURTLEBACK TILES
Designed ca. 1900–04

OPPOSITE

16 *ARROWHEAD* SHADE
Probably designed by Clara Driscoll ca. 1904

CATTAIL, POND LILY BASE
Designed ca. 1900–04

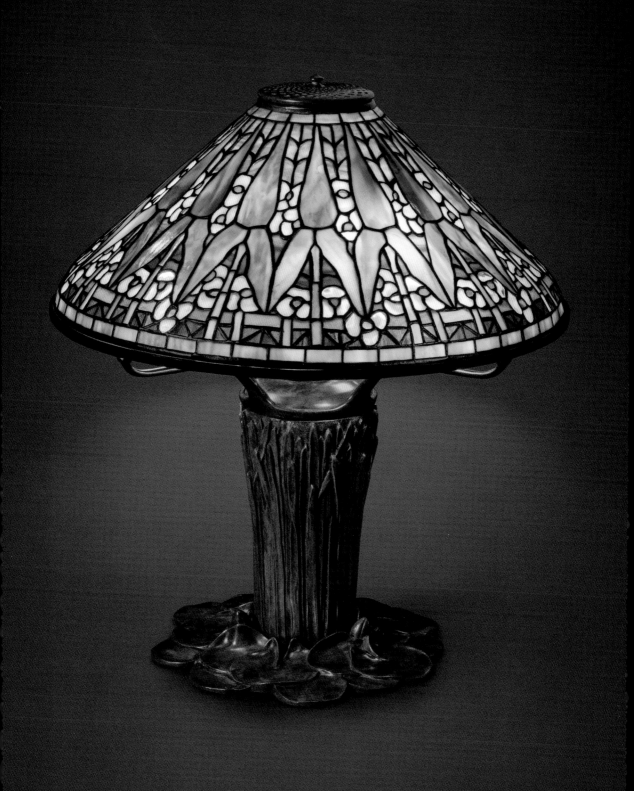

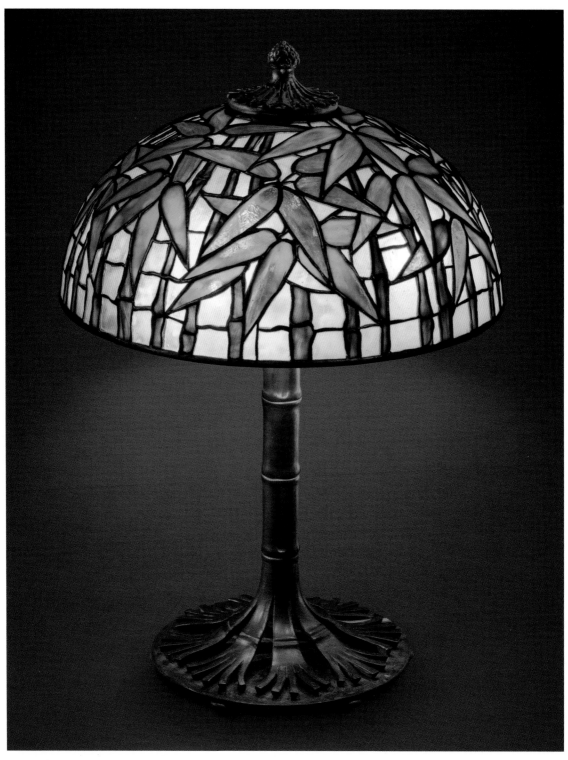

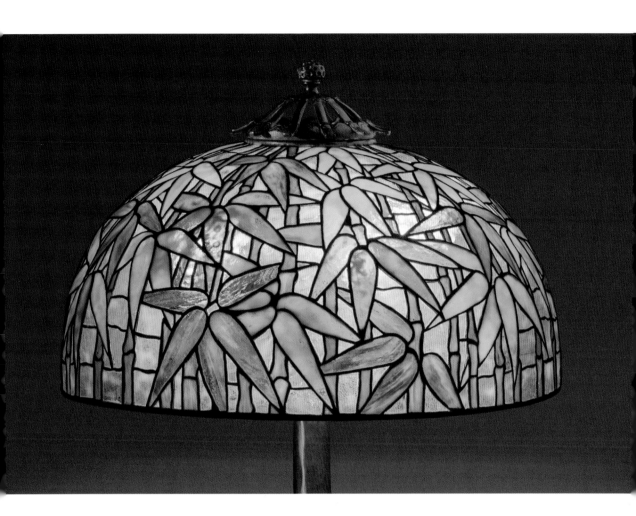

OPPOSITE

17 *BAMBOO* SHADE

Possibly designed by Clara Driscoll ca. 1900–06

BAMBOO BASE

Designed ca. 1900–06

ABOVE

18 *BAMBOO* SHADE

Possibly designed by Clara Driscoll ca. 1900–06

BAMBOO FLOOR BASE

Designed ca. 1900–06

Although there are native American species, bamboo has long been a symbol—literary, graphic, and material—for Asia, particularly China and Japan. Intense fascination with all things Japanese followed Commodore Perry's forced opening of Japan in 1854 to trade. Travelogues from the 1870s and 1880s familiarized American homes with the foreign, as did newly imported goods. The *Bamboo* shades' vertical shoots slice the dome at regular intervals, lending a graduated effect that is echoed in the branching design of the foot.

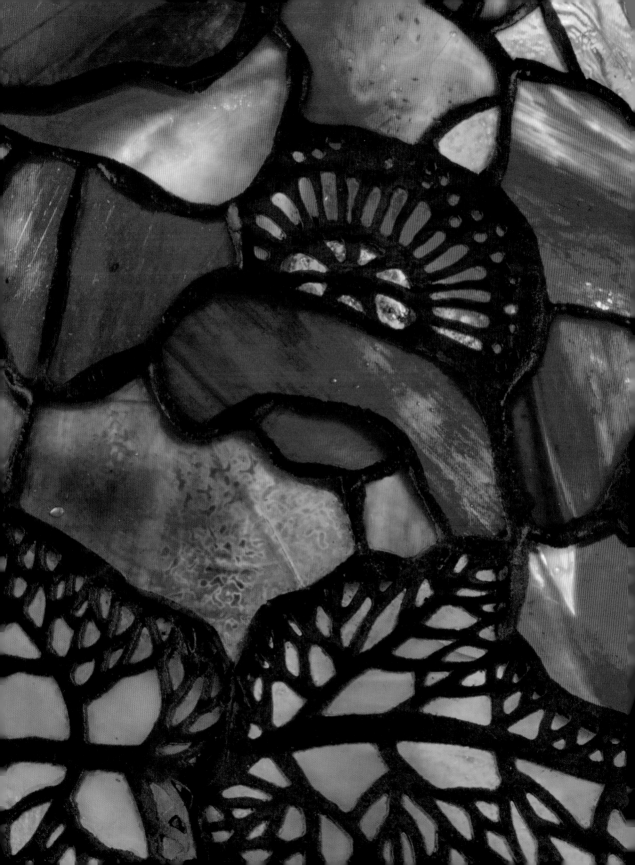

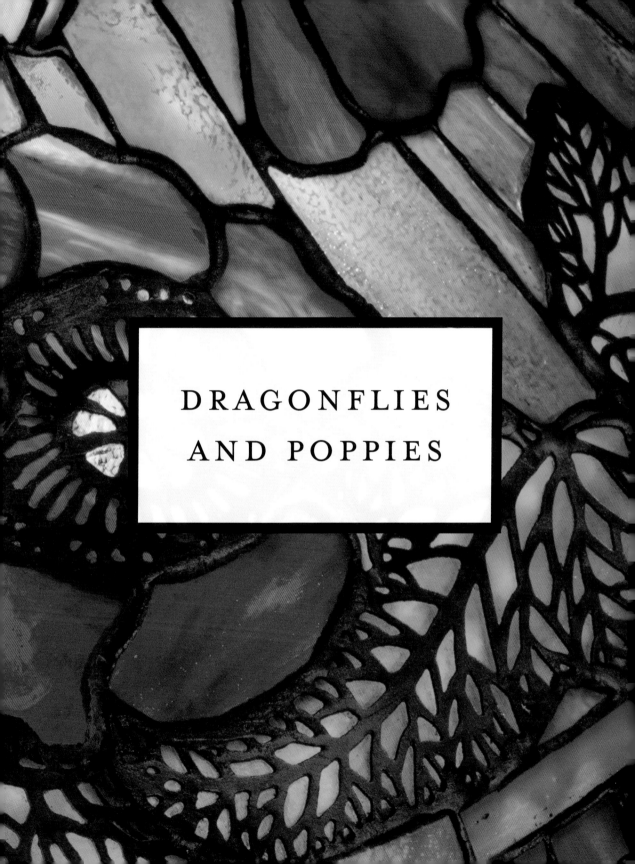

DRAGONFLIES
AND POPPIES

19 *DRAGONFLY* SHADE
Probably designed by Clara Driscoll ca. 1900–06

STANDARD BASE WITH FAVRILE GLASS BALLS
Designed ca. 1900–03

Other than Louis C. Tiffany, designers at Tiffany Studios rarely received individual public credit for their work. An exception appeared in a *New York Daily News* article in 1904, which broadcast that Clara Driscoll was responsible for the now-iconic *Dragonfly* lamp design. Distinguished by the insects' charming brass filigree wings and round, pressed-glass jewel eyes, at least five shade model variations emanated from Driscoll's first design. In this version, oval jewels effervesce through the upper section, and the lacy wings and glowing, beady eyes of dragonflies compose the edge.

PRECEDING PAGES
Detail of lamp 24

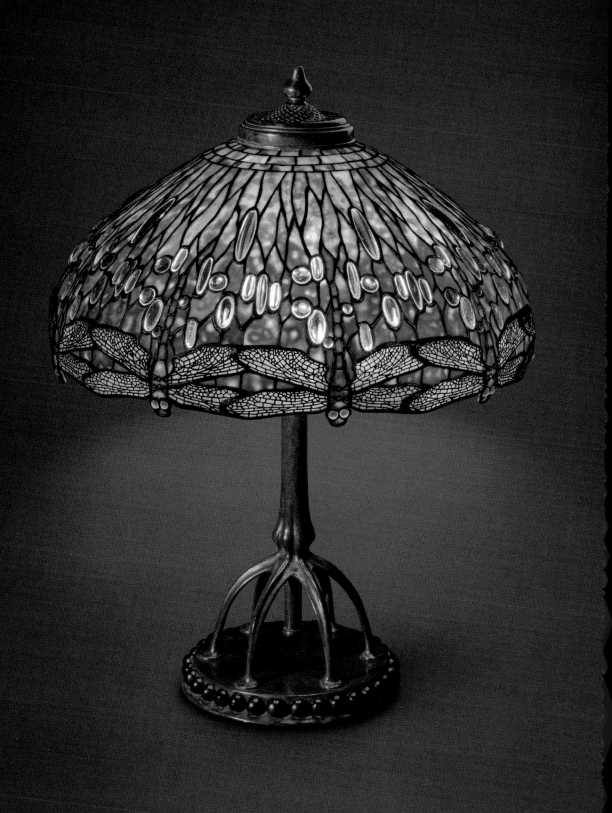

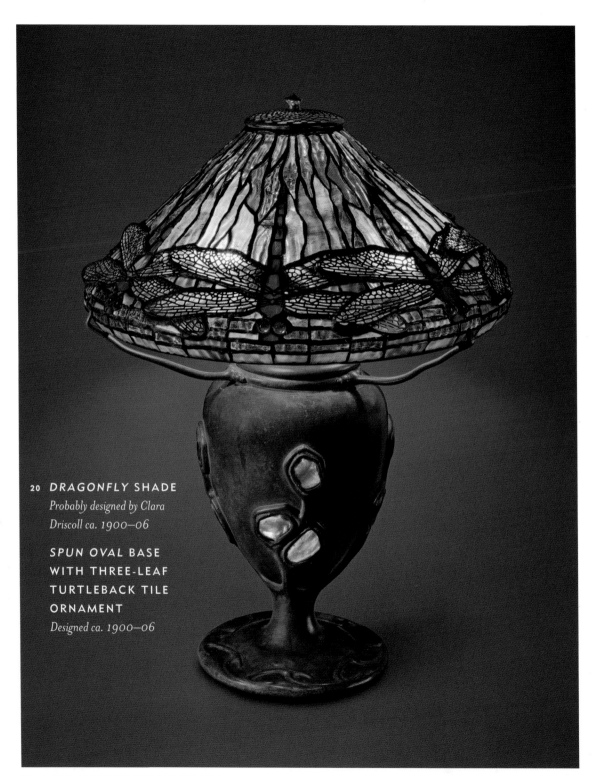

20 *DRAGONFLY SHADE*
Probably designed by Clara
Driscoll ca. 1900–06

SPUN OVAL BASE
WITH THREE-LEAF
TURTLEBACK TILE
ORNAMENT
Designed ca. 1900–06

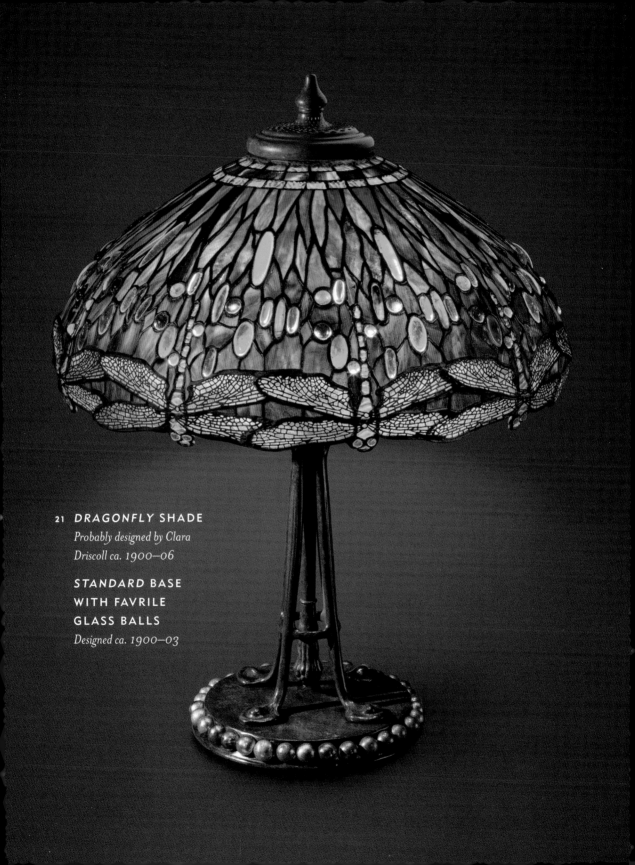

21 *DRAGONFLY* SHADE
*Probably designed by Clara
Driscoll ca. 1900–06*

STANDARD BASE
WITH FAVRILE
GLASS BALLS
Designed ca. 1900–03

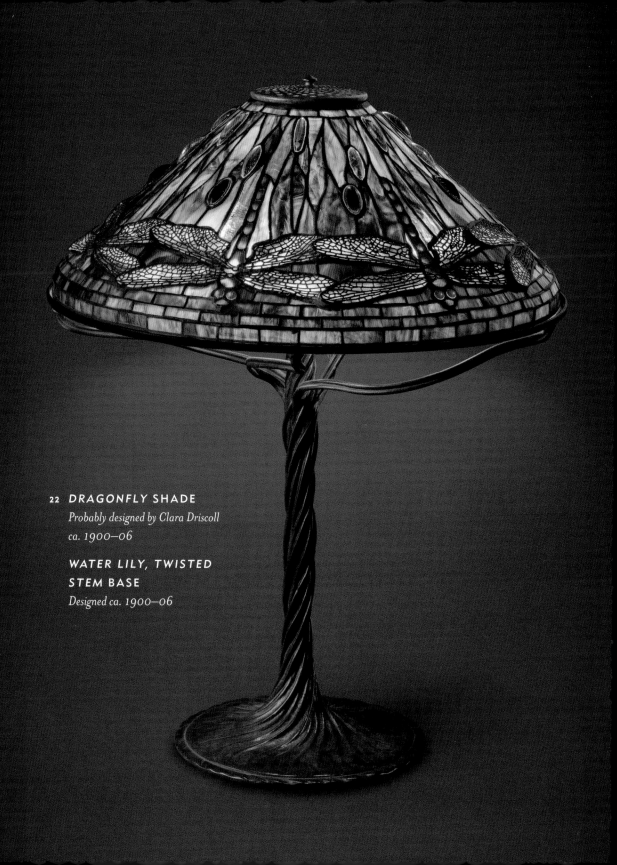

22 DRAGONFLY SHADE
Probably designed by Clara Driscoll
ca. 1900—06

WATER LILY, TWISTED STEM BASE
Designed ca. 1900—06

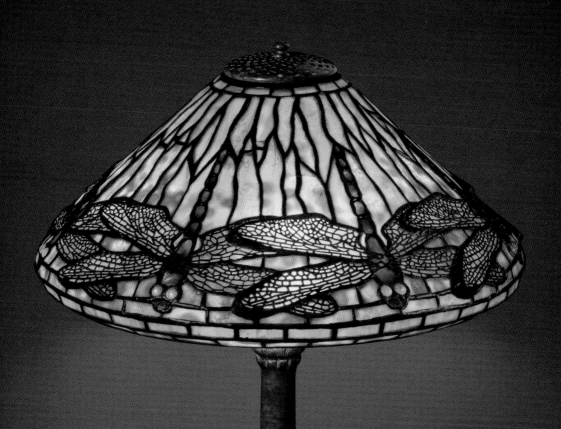

23 DRAGONFLY SHADE
Probably designed by Clara Driscoll
ca. 1900–06

**HAMMERED CUSHION
BASE**
Designed ca. 1900–06

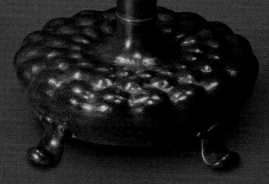

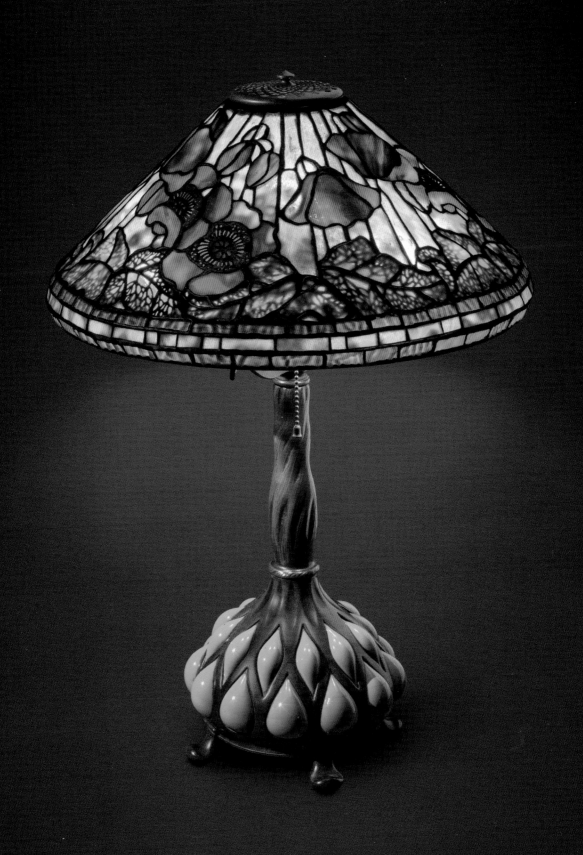

24 *POPPY* SHADE

Probably designed by Clara Driscoll ca. 1900–06

BLOWN GLASS IN METAL BASE

Designed ca. 1900–02

Textile designer Candace Wheeler, an early Tiffany collaborator and fellow
Long Island home owner, wrote in 1900 on her garden poppies at midsummer:
"I find the innumerable buds hanging their heads like shamed babies, and
never will they lift them until they are dressed and ruffled with a hundred leaves
of the silkiest silk."

Clara Driscoll does not mention the *Poppy* shade design in her correspondence.
Nonetheless, it was produced while she was head of the Women's Glass Cutting
Department and it capitalizes on her idea of brass filigree, here used to detail
the flower centers and veins of the leaves, placed over the glass or as a shadowy
underlayer. Tiffany Studios used glass plating, or layering, extensively in
its windows to blend colors or create effects of shading or depth. Given the
department's beginnings in window production, the use of layered filigree was
a short though creative step.

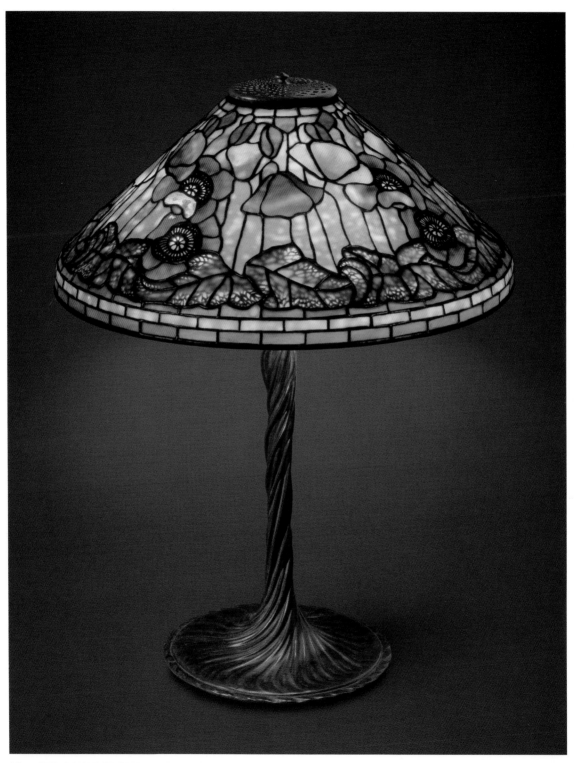

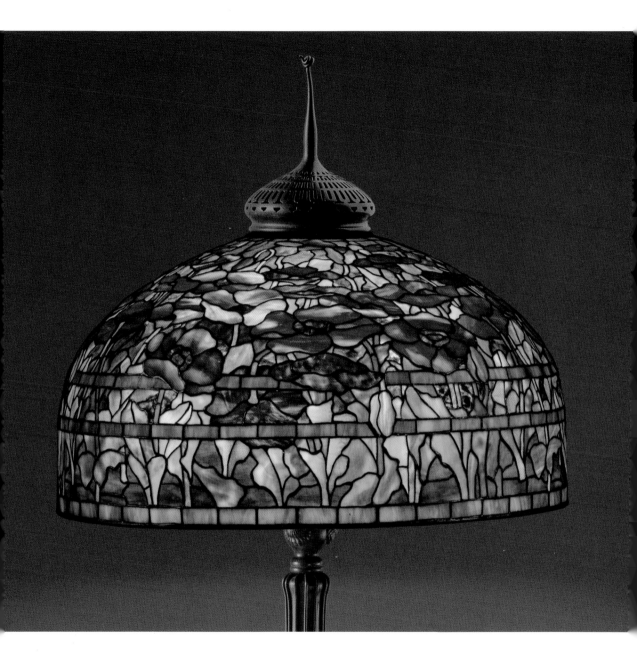

OPPOSITE

25 *POPPY* SHADE

Probably designed by Clara Driscoll ca. 1900–06

WATER LILY, TWISTED STEM BASE

Designed ca. 1900–06

ABOVE

26 *POPPY* SHADE

Possibly designed by Clara Driscoll ca. 1906–10

SCROLL FLOOR BASE

Designed ca. 1900–06

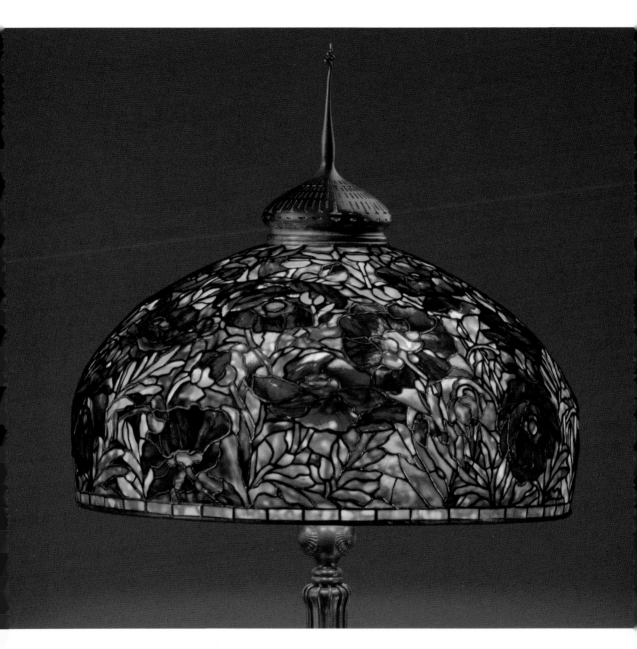

ABOVE

27 *ORIENTAL POPPY SHADE*

Designed ca. 1910—13

SCROLL FLOOR BASE

Designed ca. 1900—06

OPPOSITE

28 *POPPY SHADE*

Probably designed by Clara Driscoll ca. 1900—06

RIBBED CUSHION BASE

Designed ca. 1900—02

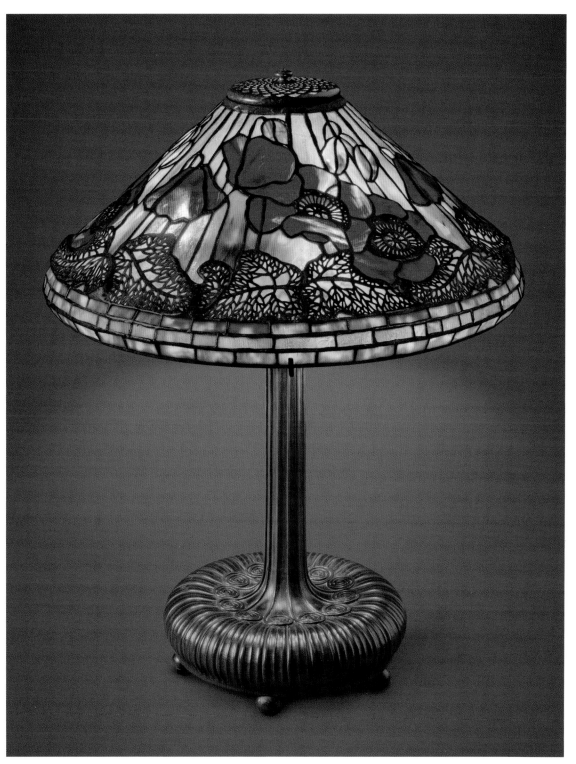

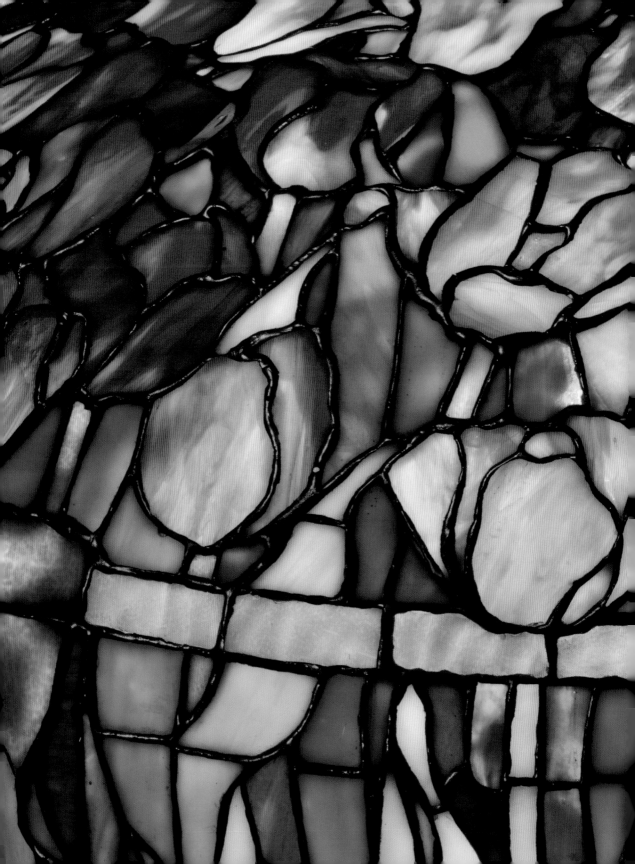

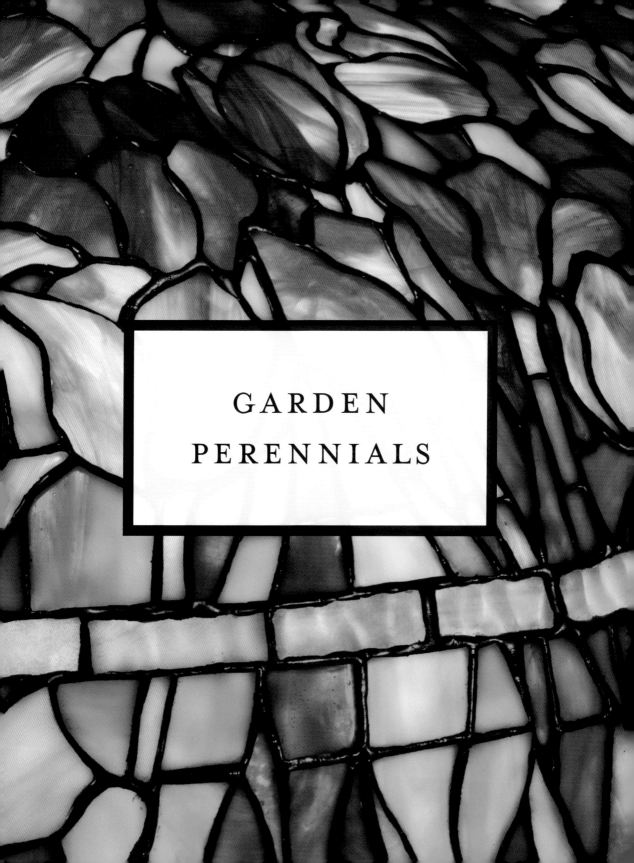

GARDEN
PERENNIALS

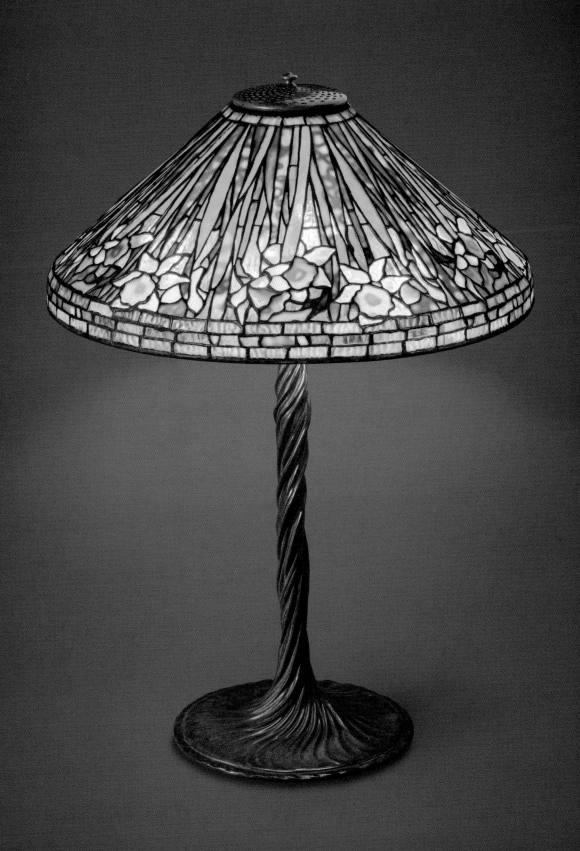

29 *DAFFODIL* SHADE
Probably designed by Clara Driscoll ca. 1900–06

WATER LILY, TWISTED STEM BASE
Designed ca. 1900–06

Tiffany Studios designers were avid students of nature. Louis C. Tiffany regularly supplied them with cuttings from his gardens, and they referred to an in-house library of illustrated books and photographs. An archival photograph depicting long-stemmed cut daffodils laid on a paper cone, downwardly arranged as in the *Daffodil* shade design, indicates a direct design process for this model. The positions of the glass mottles in the flowers cleverly indicate the trumpets.

According to Tiffany's personal aesthetics, daffodils as a lamp theme would inspire instinctive feelings of happiness. "Our hereditary need is for an artificial light which shall be slightly yellow," he wrote in 1911 for *Scientific American*. "Yellow is the color of brightness and mirth. Through hereditary association of ideas yellow suggests to the mind the idea of brightness, brilliancy, or sunshine."

PRECEDING PAGES
Detail of lamp 34

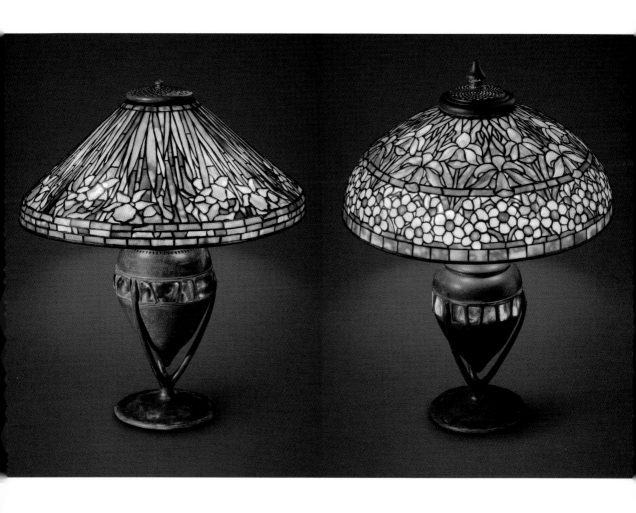

30 *DAFFODIL* SHADE

    Probably designed by Clara Driscoll ca. 1900–06

CRUTCH OVAL BASE WITH
TURTLEBACK TILE BAND

    Designed ca. 1900–06

31 *DAFFODIL AND NARCISSUS* SHADE

    Designed ca. 1910–13

CRUTCH OVAL BASE WITH
TURTLEBACK TILE BAND

    Designed ca. 1900–06

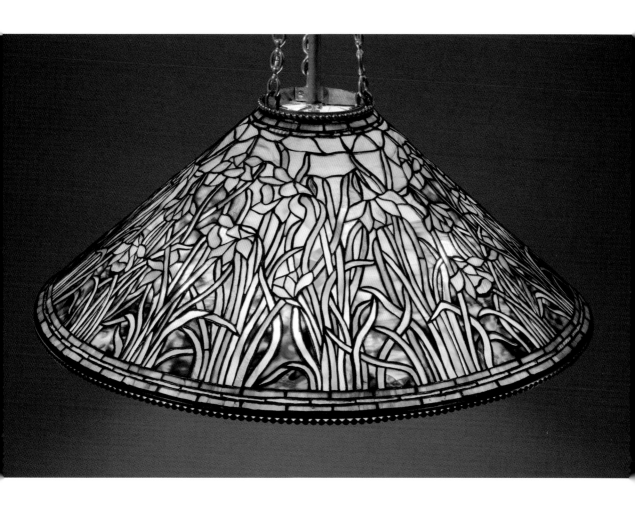

32 *DAFFODIL* HANGING SHADE

Probably designed by Clara Driscoll ca. 1900—06

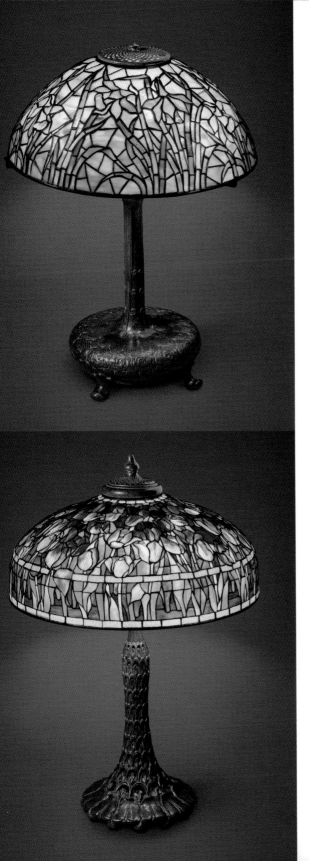

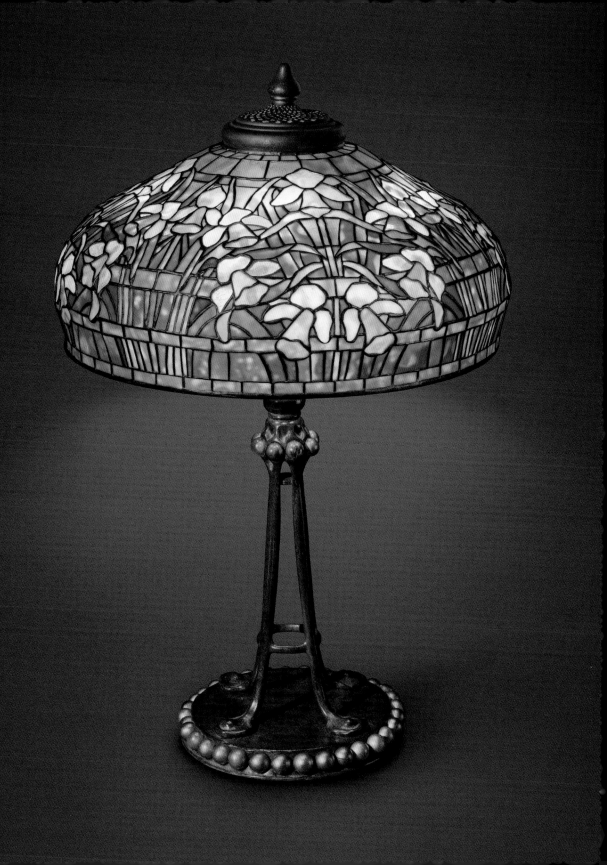

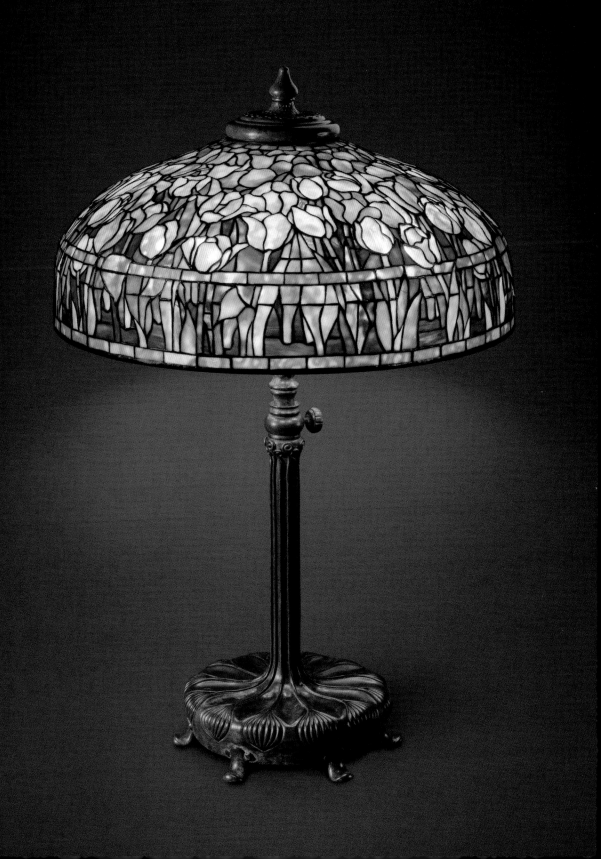

36 *TULIP* SHADE

Possibly designed by Clara Driscoll ca. 1906–10

POD CUSHION BASE

Designed ca. 1900–03

Tulips, which are native to Central Asia, are strongly linked with the
Netherlands thanks to their starring role in a speculative mania for the bulbs
during the early seventeenth century. Dutch American heritage festivals
often center on the tulip's flowering period. Advising turn-of-the-century
American gardeners, Tiffany's early collaborator Candace Wheeler wrote,
"It is as easy to buy by the thousand as by the dozen, and a certain sentiment
will attach itself to a thousand tulip bulbs, which you know were grown on
the mud flats of Holland, tended by slow and heavy men in blue blouses." In
planting them, "you can see in your mind the flattened fields of their nativity,
covered with millions of blossoming tulips." Such a teeming field covers the
Tulip shade, in which a dense crowd of colorful blooms gathers above the stem-
filled apron.

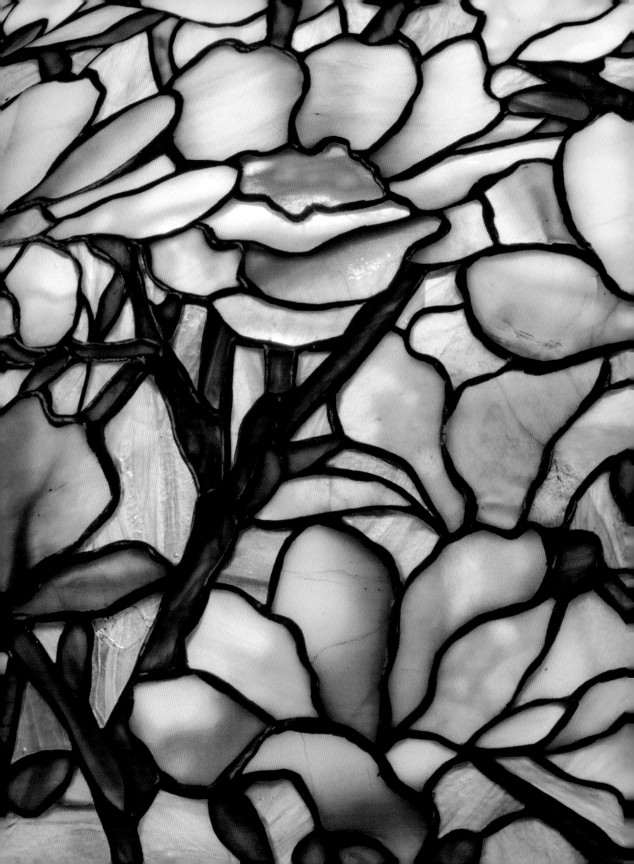

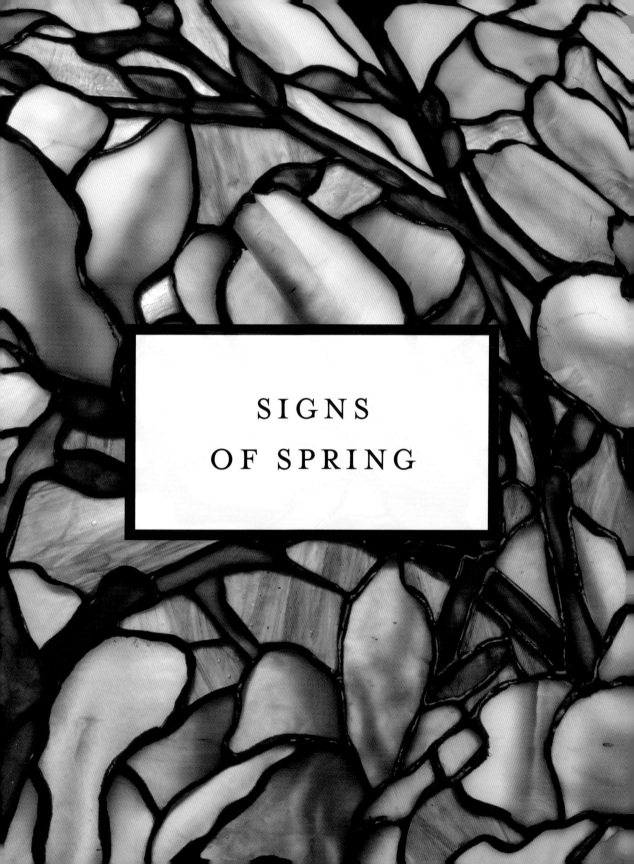

SIGNS

OF SPRING

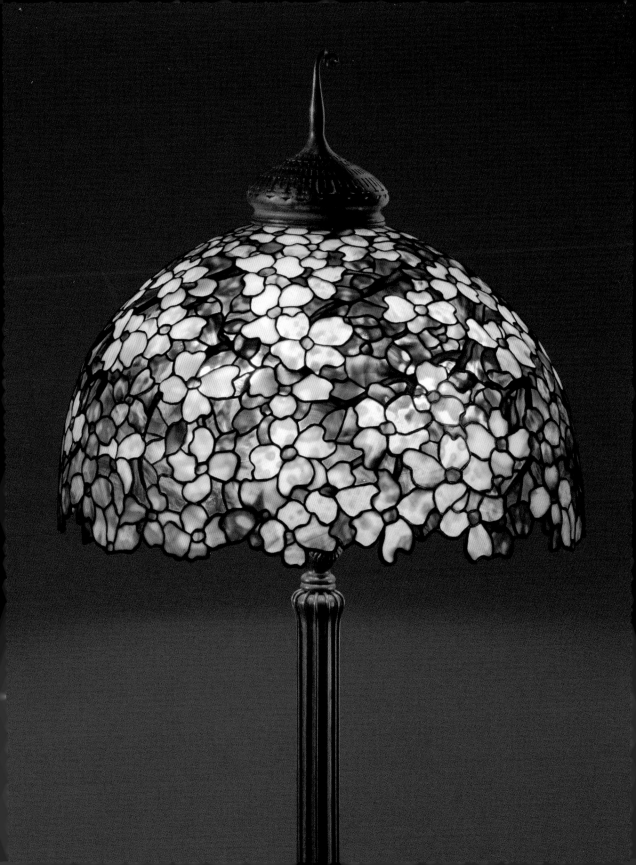

37 *DOGWOOD* SHADE

Probably designed by Clara Driscoll ca. 1900–06

CHASED POD FLOOR BASE

Designed ca. 1900–06

Native to North America, the flowering dogwood contains quinine in its bark, and so has a long history as a home remedy. Its showy "flowers," which overtake the trees in May, are really composed of four white bracts, or modified leaves, surrounding a cluster of tiny blossoms. The *Dogwood* shade renders the central cluster as an indistinct color mass. The mottled glass used for the bracts reinforces the telltale notches at their tips.

PRECEDING PAGES
Detail of lamp 40

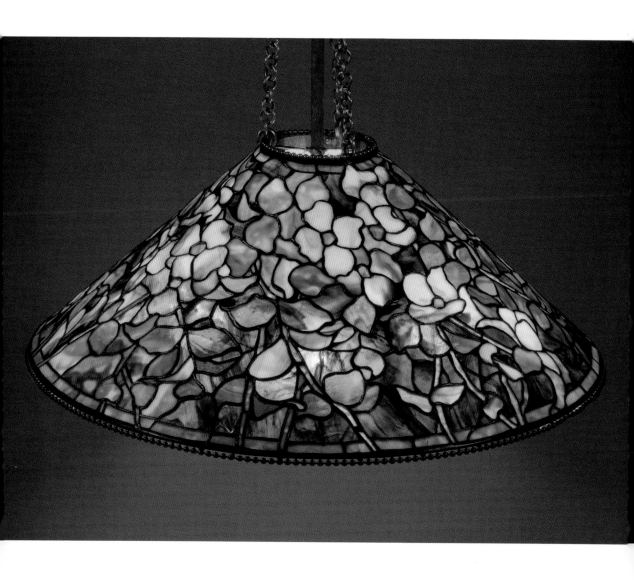

38 *DOGWOOD* HANGING SHADE

Probably designed by Clara Driscoll ca. 1900–06

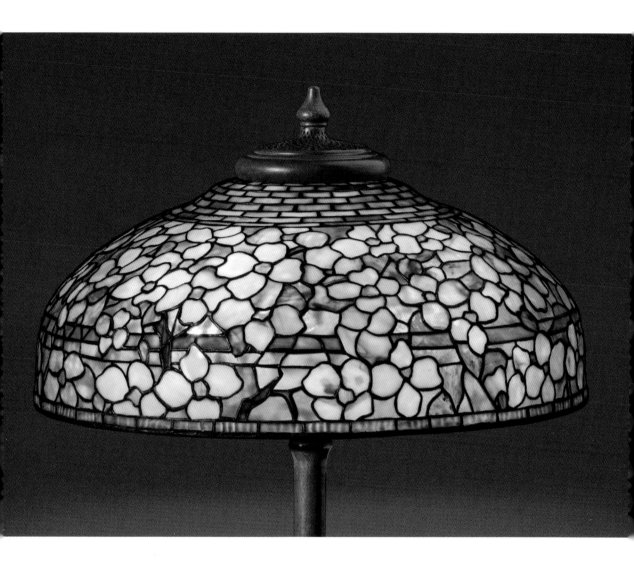

39 *DOGWOOD* SHADE

Probably designed by Clara Driscoll ca. 1900–06

PIANO FLOOR BASE

Designed ca. 1900–06

40 *MAGNOLIA* SHADE

Possibly designed by Clara Driscoll ca. 1906–10

CHASED POD FLOOR BASE

Designed ca. 1900–06

By the time the *Magnolia* shade appeared on the 1910 *Price List*, five leaded glass *Magnolia* window panels had graced the library of the Louis C. Tiffany house at East Seventy-second Street, New York City, for about twenty-five years. Yet the motif's appeal endured for Tiffany Studios and its clients. "Drapery" glass, which was folded while semimolten, gives luscious substance to the flowers' thick petals. First created to mimic the drapery of garments in figural windows, this innovation and others grew out of Tiffany's goal of minimizing, if not eliminating, the traditional reliance on enamel paints for shading flesh and clothing in stained glass. Instead, he modulated the glass colors, textures, and thicknesses. Privileging structure over surface—intrinsic qualities over applied ornament—reflects the "truth to materials" dictate that design reformers championed from the mid-nineteenth century onward.

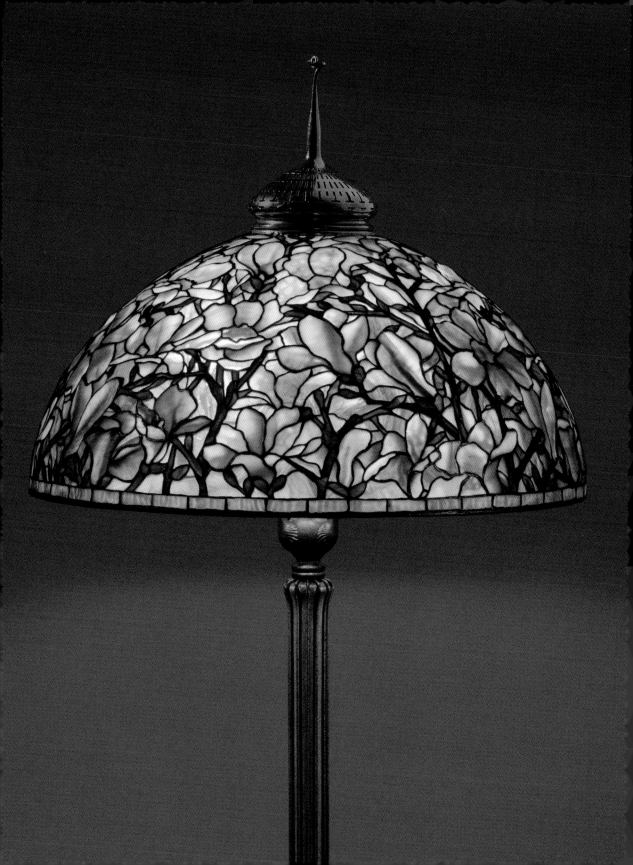

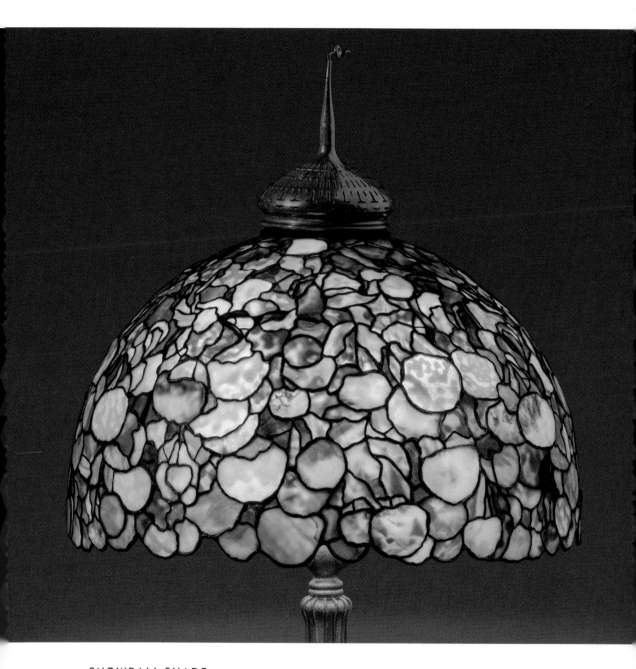

41 *SNOWBALL SHADE*

Probably designed by Clara Driscoll ca. 1900–06

FLOOR BASE

Designed ca. 1900–06

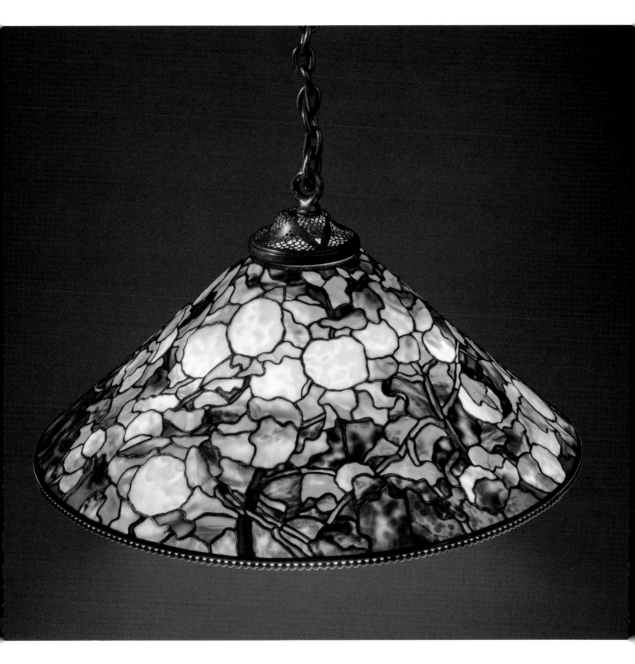

42 *SNOWBALL* HANGING SHADE

Probably designed by Clara Driscoll ca. 1900–06

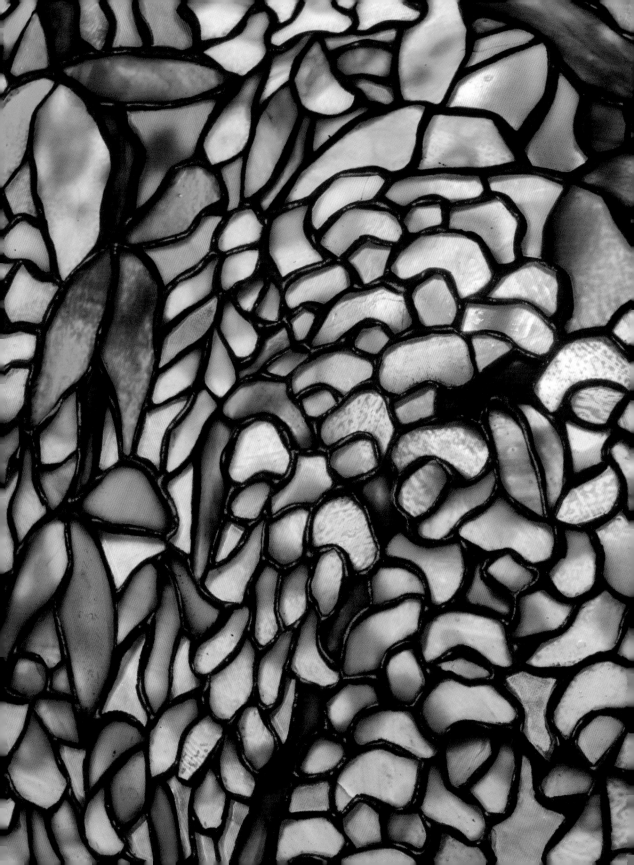

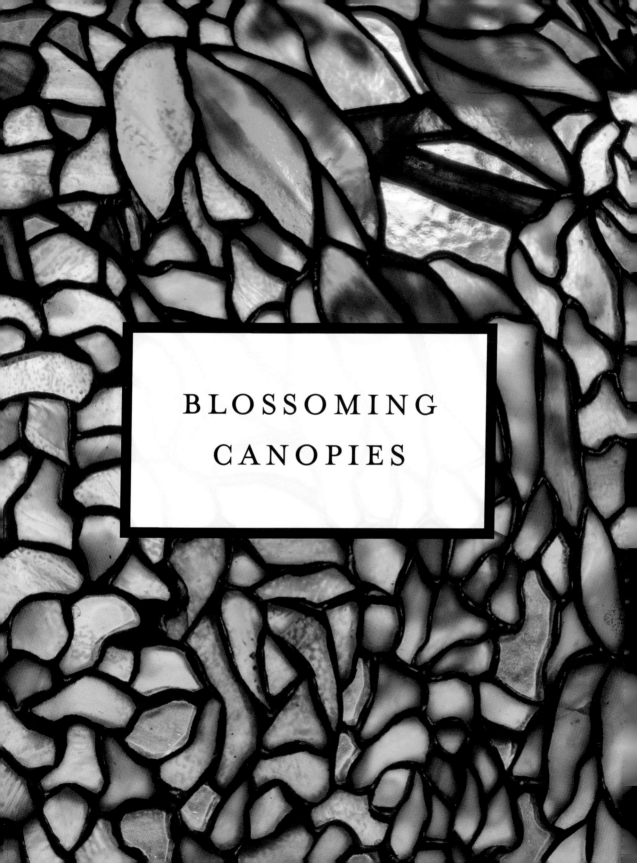

BLOSSOMING
CANOPIES

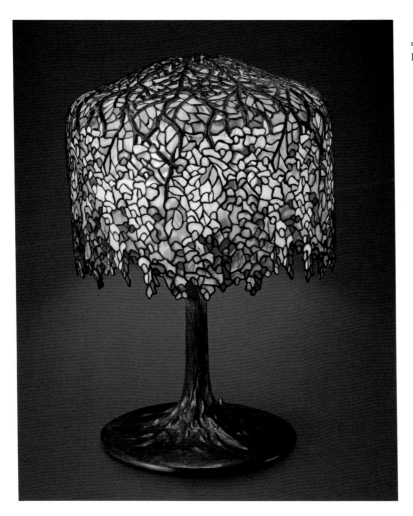

43 *WISTERIA* TABLE LAMP

Designed by Clara Driscoll ca. 1901

Wisteria abounded in Tiffany's leaded glass windows and also on the grounds of Laurelton Hall, where they were encouraged to drape over purpose-built canopies as if they were flowering portieres or valances. Their pendulous flower clusters softened the margins between indoors and out. Historians previously attributed the *Wisteria* lamp to Mrs. Curtis Freshel, a Tiffany Studios client living in Boston, but now understand it to be the work of Clara Driscoll. The shade's two thousand pieces of glass were assembled upon a wooden block shape that would provide the form of the *Apple Blossom*, *Grape*, and *Trumpet Creeper*, each paired with the same treelike base.

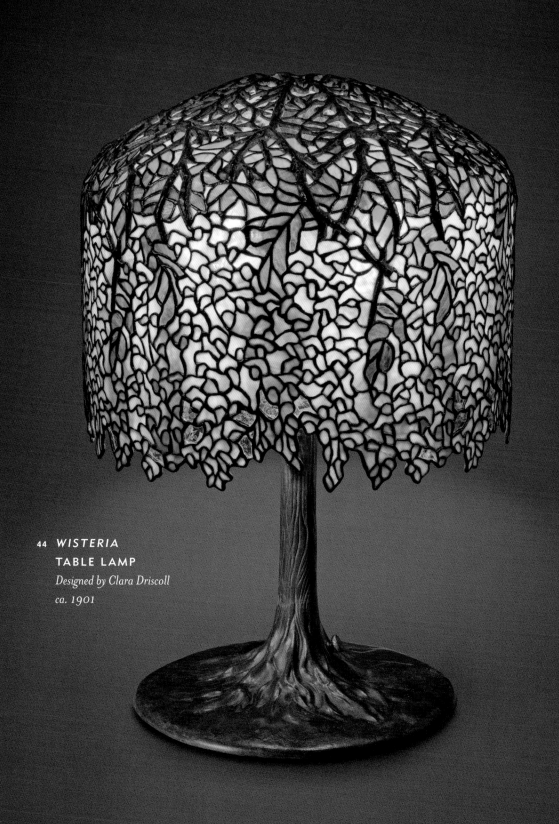

44 *WISTERIA*
TABLE LAMP

Designed by Clara Driscoll
ca. 1901

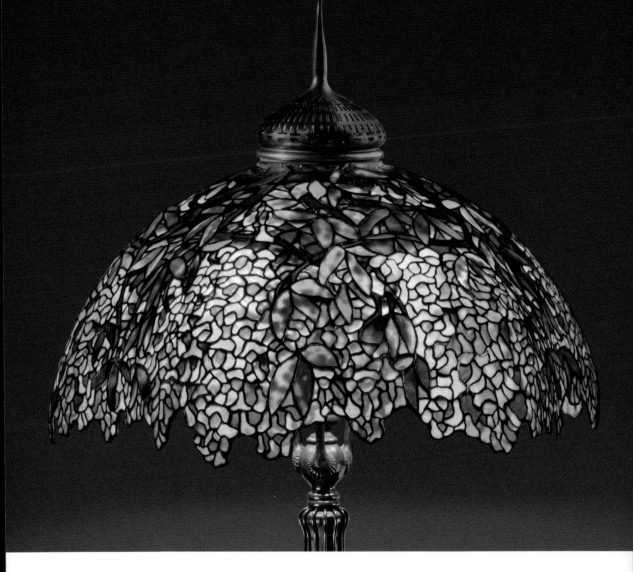

45 *LABURNUM* SHADE

Probably designed by Clara Driscoll ca. 1901–06

SCROLL FLOOR BASE

Designed ca. 1900–06

46 *LABURNUM* SHADE

Probably designed by Clara Driscoll ca. 1901–06

BIRD SKELETON BASE

Designed ca. 1900–06

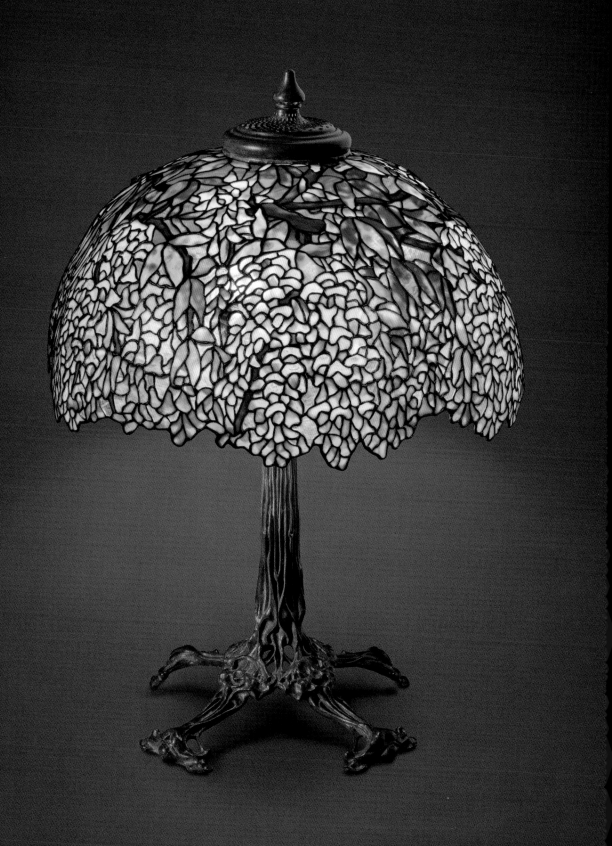

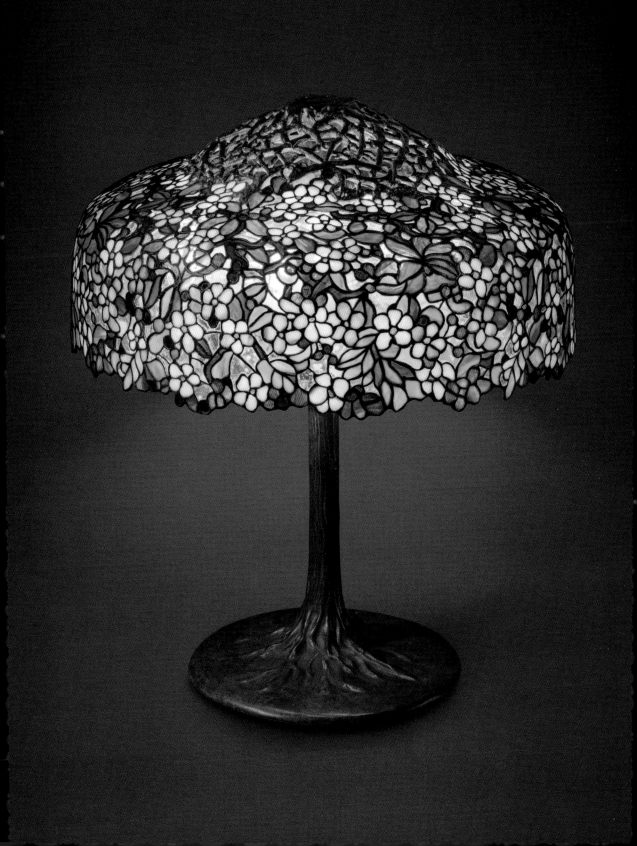

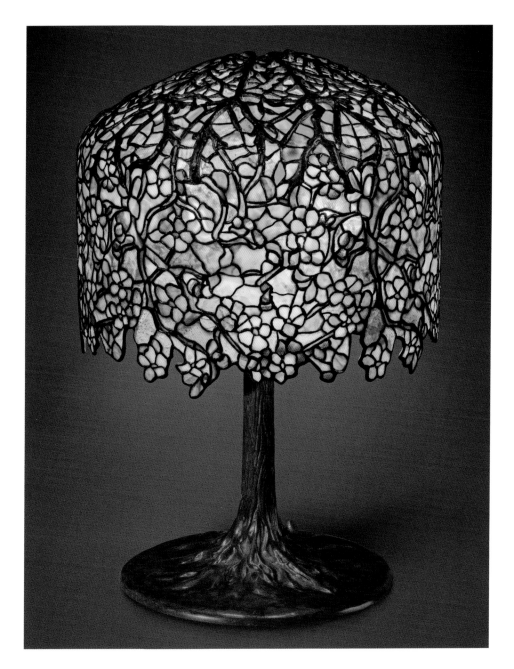

47 *APPLE BLOSSOM* TABLE LAMP

Probably designed by Clara Driscoll ca. 1901–06

48 *APPLE BLOSSOM* TABLE LAMP

Probably designed by Clara Driscoll ca. 1901–06

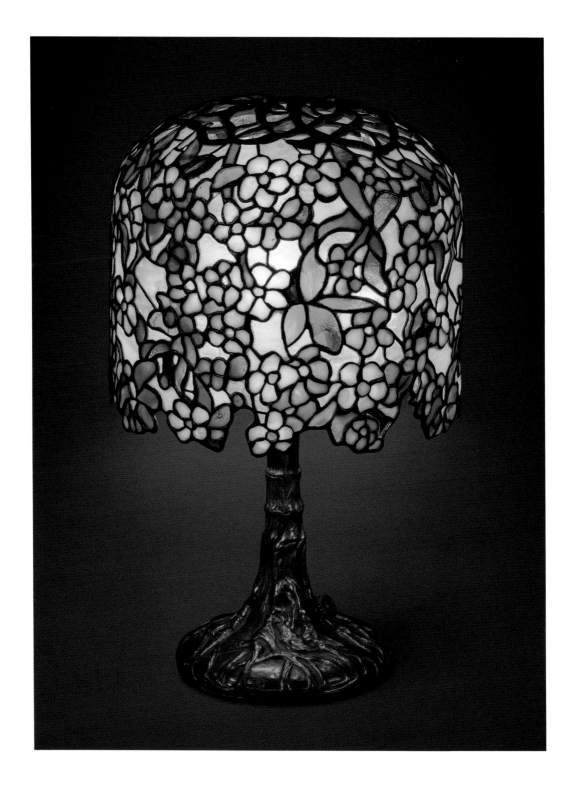

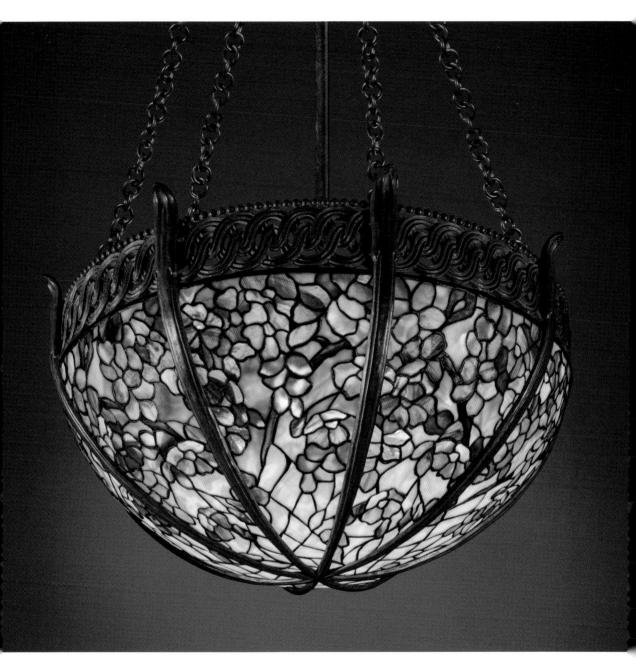

49 *PONY APPLE BLOSSOM*
TABLE LAMP

Probably designed by Clara Driscoll ca. 1901–06

50 *APPLE BLOSSOM*
HANGING SHADE

Designed ca. 1910

51 *COBWEB* SHADE, *MOSAIC FLORAL* BASE
Designed by Clara Driscoll ca. 1902

Early in his career, Tiffany designed wallpapers for Warren, Fuller & Co. that were published in Clarence Cook's 1880 book *What Shall We Do with Our Walls?* One featured cobwebs spun within clematis foliage, echoed in the way they splay among apple blossoms in Clara Driscoll's *Cobweb* lamp. American aesthetes admired the Japanese cobweb motif. As the New York–based humor magazine *Puck* cheekily reported in 1889, the "stork is not everything in Japanese art. The latest novelty in this picturesque line is the silken cobweb." While a woman would be dismayed at finding a naturally occurring cobweb in her house, one "that costs money and is a thing of beauty, is very different. Every one will go into raptures over it." *Cobweb*, with its puzzle-fitted *Mosaic Floral* fuel base, certainly cost money. In 1906, it retailed for $500—the same price as a Ford Model N car, released that year.

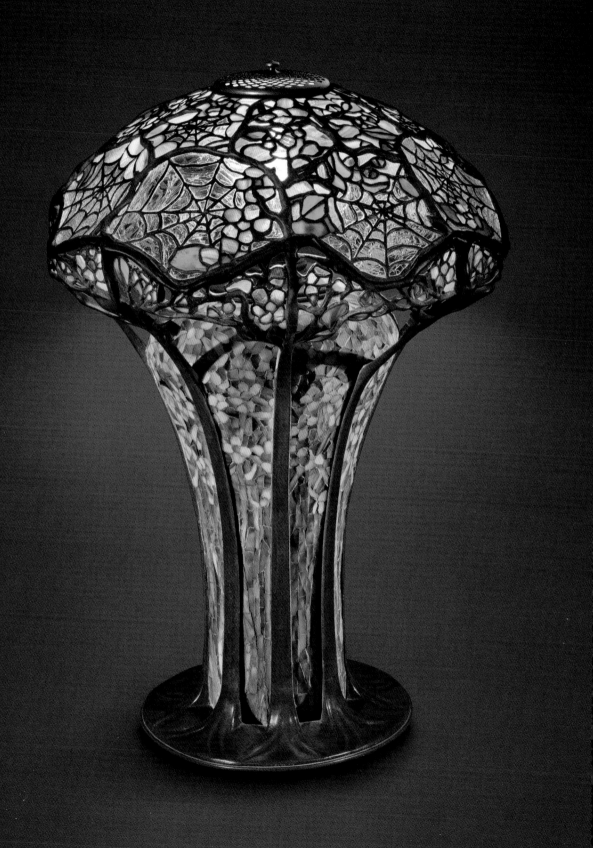

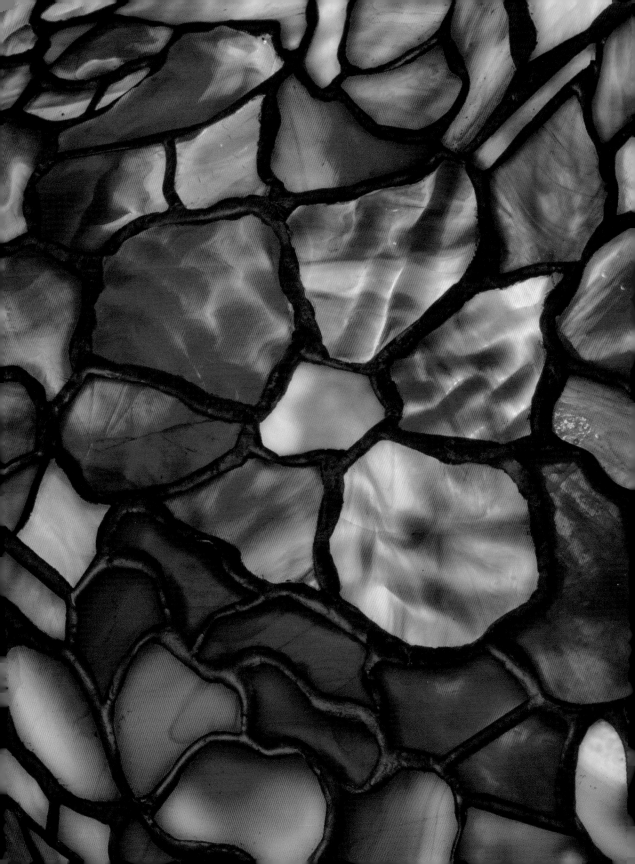

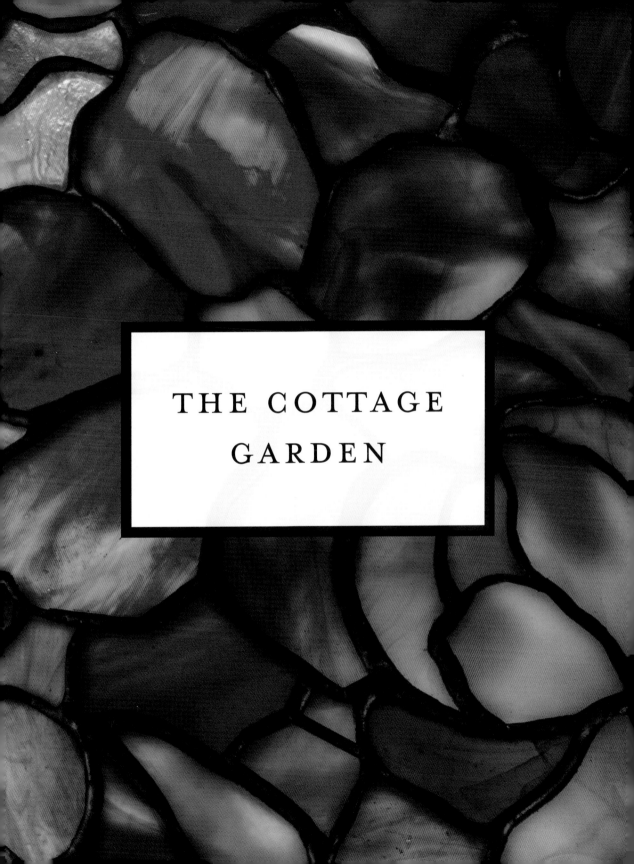

THE COTTAGE
GARDEN

52 *CYCLAMEN* SHADE

Probably designed by Clara Driscoll ca. 1900–06

LEAF CUSHION BASE

Designed ca. 1900–02

The late nineteenth-century English gardener William Robinson exerted tremendous influence on landscape design through his challenges to formalism. In *The Wild Garden* (1870), he advocated a "naturalized" appearance using large drifts of flowers and grasses, and perennial and native plants over carpet beds and exotics. He also paid renewed attention to the English cottage garden. His ideas, and those of garden designer Gertrude Jekyll, found favor with transatlantic Arts and Crafts audiences and artists in general, including American Impressionist painters. While cyclamen are from the Mediterranean, not England, Robinson liked their hardy adaptability. The petite scale of the *Cyclamen* shade recalls the flower's frequent use as a potted houseplant.

PRECEDING PAGES
Detail of lamp 61

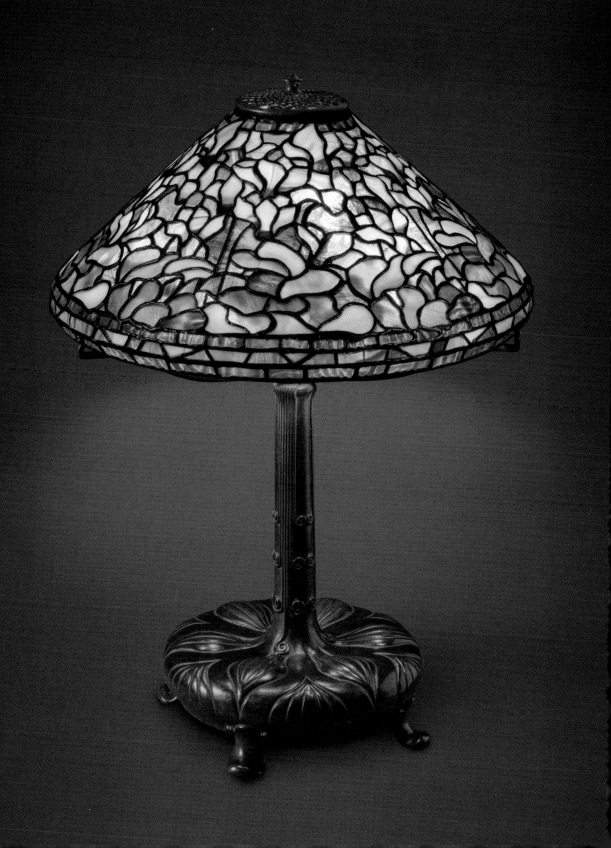

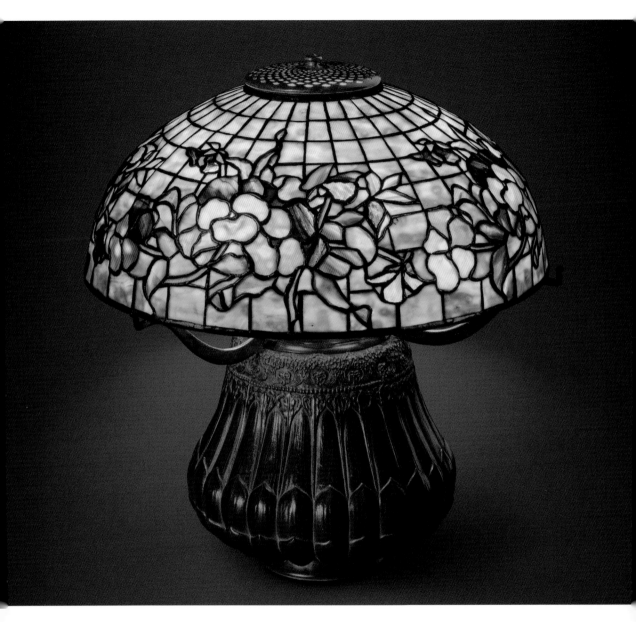

ABOVE

53 *PANSY* SHADE

Probably designed by Clara Driscoll ca. 1900—06

NIGHT BLOOMING CEREUS BASE

Designed ca. 1900—02

OPPOSITE

54 *BLACK-EYED SUSAN* SHADE

Probably designed by Clara Driscoll ca. 1900—06

SPUN OVAL BASE WITH THREE-LEAF
TURTLEBACK TILE ORNAMENT

Designed ca. 1900—06

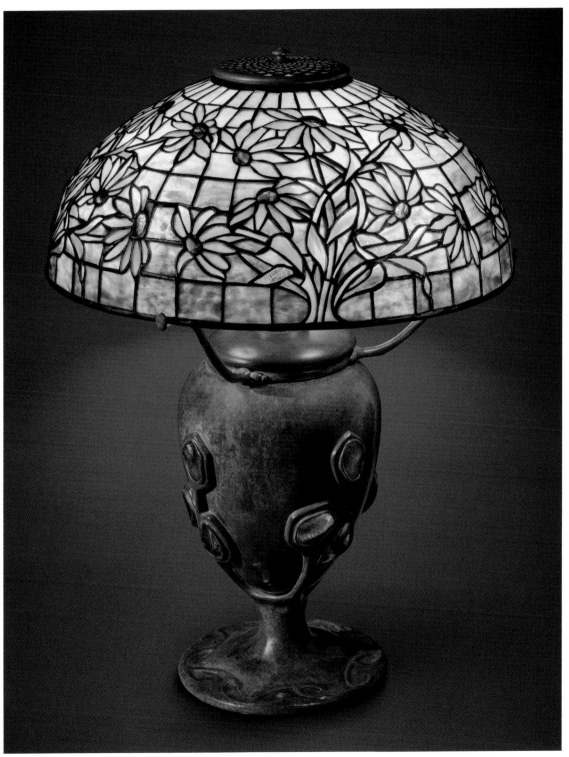

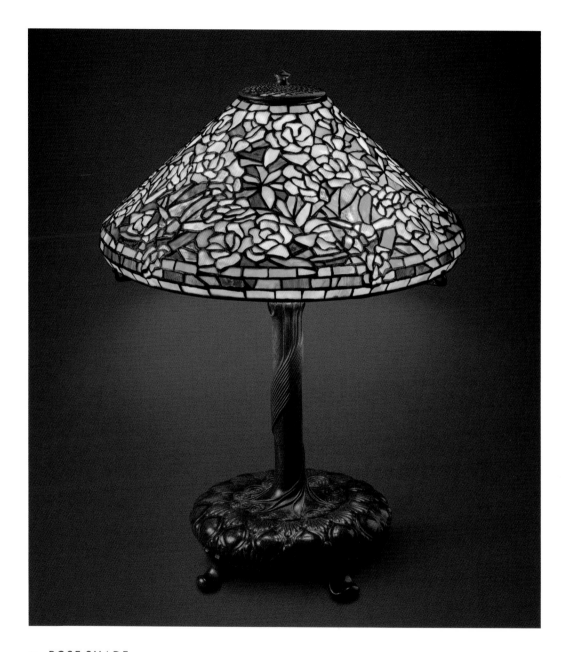

55 *ROSE* SHADE

Probably designed by Clara Driscoll ca. 1900–06

CONVENTIONAL CUSHION BASE

Designed ca. 1900–06

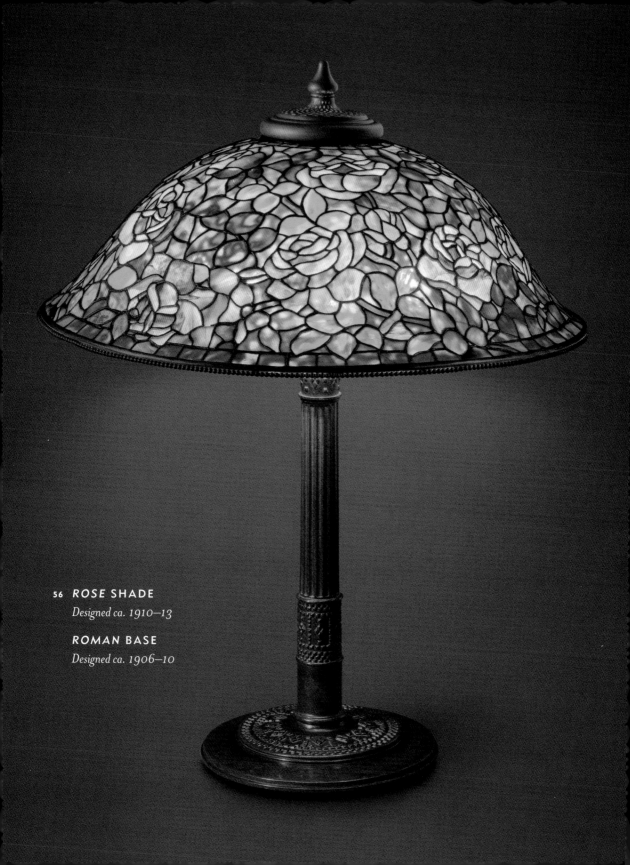

56 ROSE SHADE
Designed ca. 1910–13

ROMAN BASE
Designed ca. 1906–10

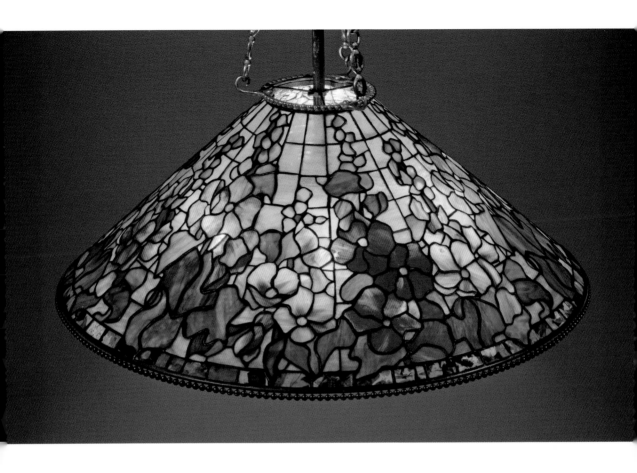

57 *HOLLYHOCK* HANGING SHADE

Probably designed by Clara Driscoll ca. 1900–06

American interest in cottage gardens coincided with the rise of nativist Colonial Revivalism. Writers nostalgically recast the idea of informal, idyllic garden spaces as "old-fashioned" and "old-time." Many of the favored plants characterized the traditional English cottage garden rather than being native species, but admirers of the style relished the idea that colonists may have brought the seeds. In 1901 popular historian Alice Morse Earle wrote, "I think we may safely affirm that the Hollyhock is the most popular, and most widely known, of all old-fashioned flowers. It is loved for its beauty, its associations, its adaptiveness."

Lush, vibrant informal gardens were a frequent subject in late nineteenth- and early twentieth-century American paintings, which often depicted hollyhocks towering over people. An appropriate theme for a chandelier, the plant, with its remarkable height—they grow up to six feet tall—is given its due in the *Hollyhock* shade.

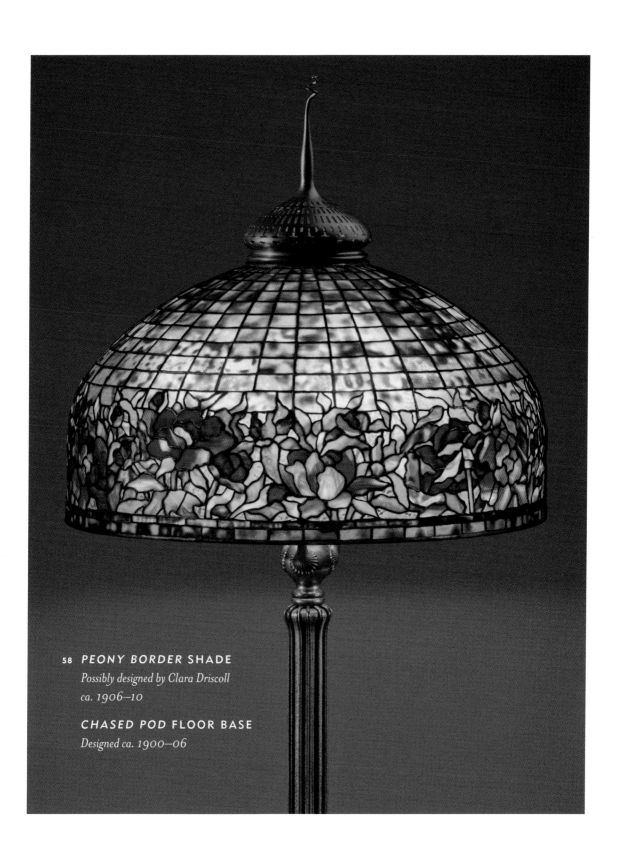

58 *PEONY BORDER* SHADE
Possibly designed by Clara Driscoll
ca. 1906–10

CHASED POD FLOOR BASE
Designed ca. 1900–06

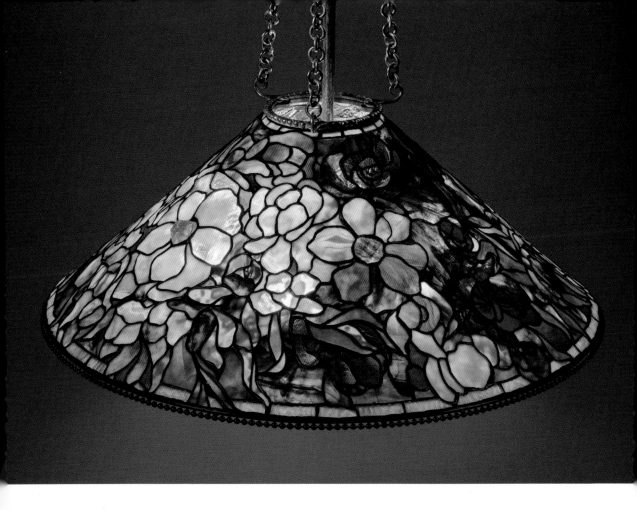

59 *PEONY* HANGING SHADE

Probably designed by Clara Driscoll ca. 1900–04

Tiffany's Laurelton Hall included a "grandmother's garden," yet another term for the
Colonial Revival "old-time" garden. In one of his several published accounts of Tiffany's
residences, Samuel Howe, a former Tiffany employee turned magazine writer, fawned
over the Laurelton grounds, describing "wide borders of flowers, the big beds of poppies,
peonies, morning-glories, larkspur, dahlias, candytuft, London pride, bouncing-bet and
the whole host of old-time favorites, each in their separate bed." The glass selection in this
Peony shade imparts a painterly quality, much like that favored by cottage garden enthusiasts.
Though chunky jewels had been among Tiffany materials since about 1880, their use as
the center of one of the somewhat naturalistic flowers gives a raw beauty to the shade, which
might have seemed avant-garde at the time (see detail page 2).

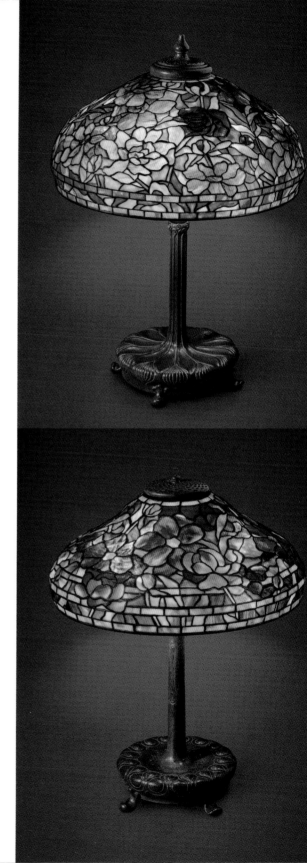

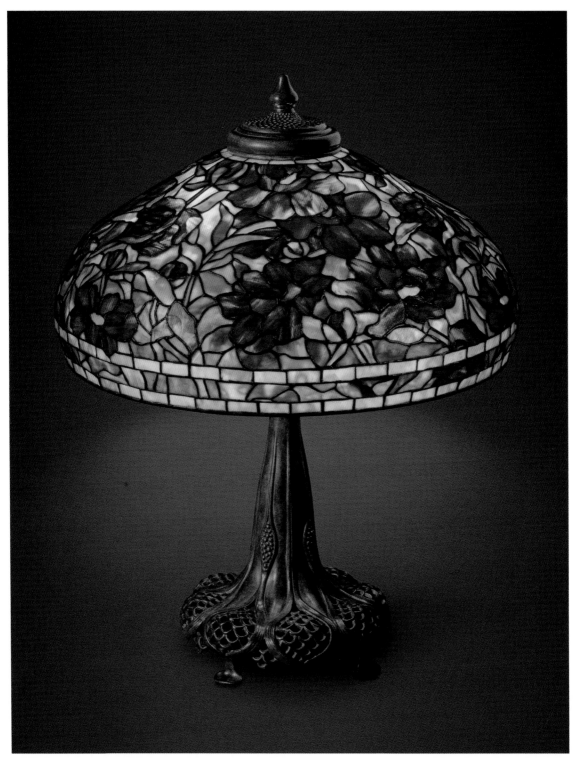

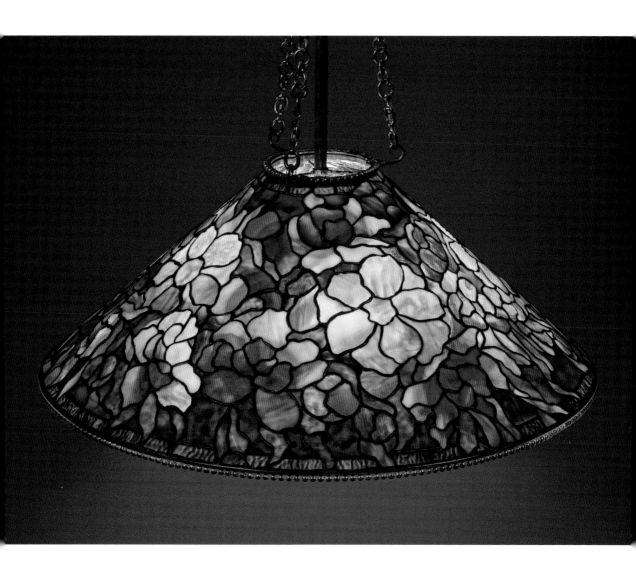

62 *PEONY* SHADE

Probably designed by Clara Driscoll ca. 1900—04

LIBRARY STANDARD BASE

Designed ca. 1900—06

63 *PEONY* HANGING SHADE

Probably designed by Clara Driscoll ca. 1900—04

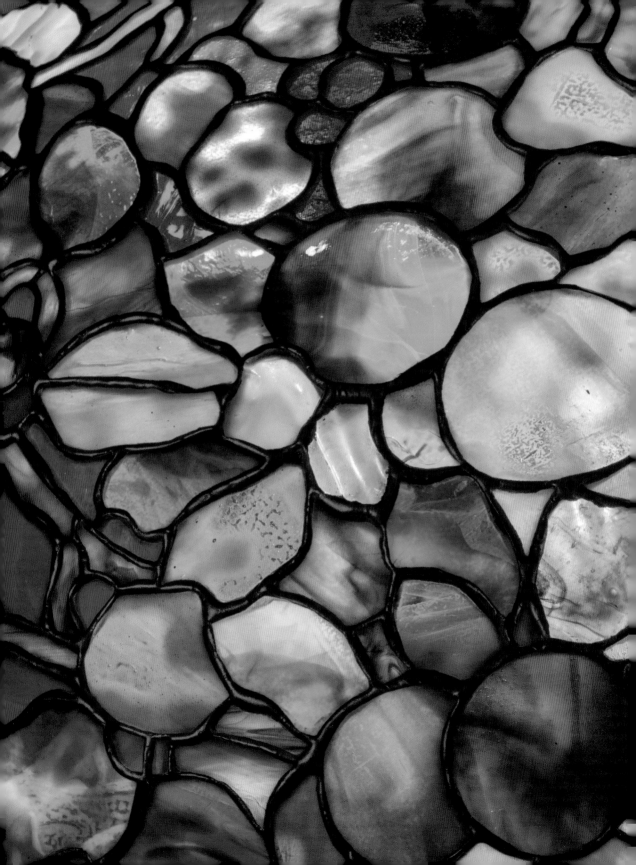

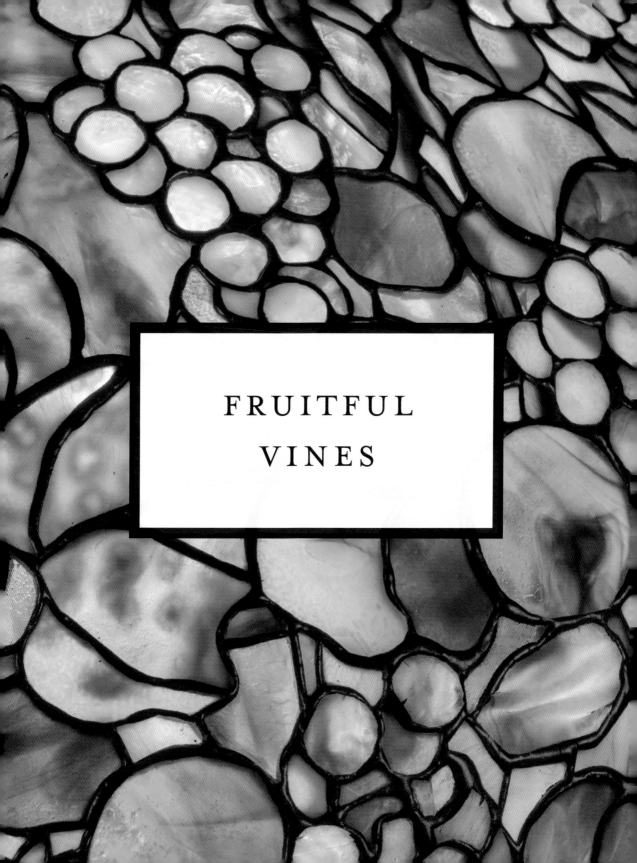

FRUITFUL VINES

64 *FRUIT* SHADE

Probably designed by Clara Driscoll ca. 1900–06

BRONZE POTTERY BASE

Designed ca. 1908

Louis C. Tiffany seems to have enjoyed the idea of bucolic agrarian abundance and human connection to seasonal cycles. There was farming life at Laurelton Hall, including cattle and an apple orchard, but he was more a gentleman farmer than a serious producer. Many of his contemporaries hailed the benefits of rural living in the face of America's rapid urbanization, and Tiffany Studios often advertised in *Country Life in America* magazine, a major advocate of the lifestyle to its affluent audience. *Fruit* depicts a cornucopia of grapes and round fruits that change character depending on coloration. One half of this particular example uses an ultrasaturated palette, while the other side is much paler, demonstrating the artistic possibilities available to glass selectors (see detail on preceding pages).

The Japanesque gourd-shaped base with maple leaves in low relief is an example of Favrile bronze pottery, which was electroplated with copper and patinated to resemble bronze. Tiffany Studios applied the technique primarily to vases.

PRECEDING PAGES
Detail of lamp 64

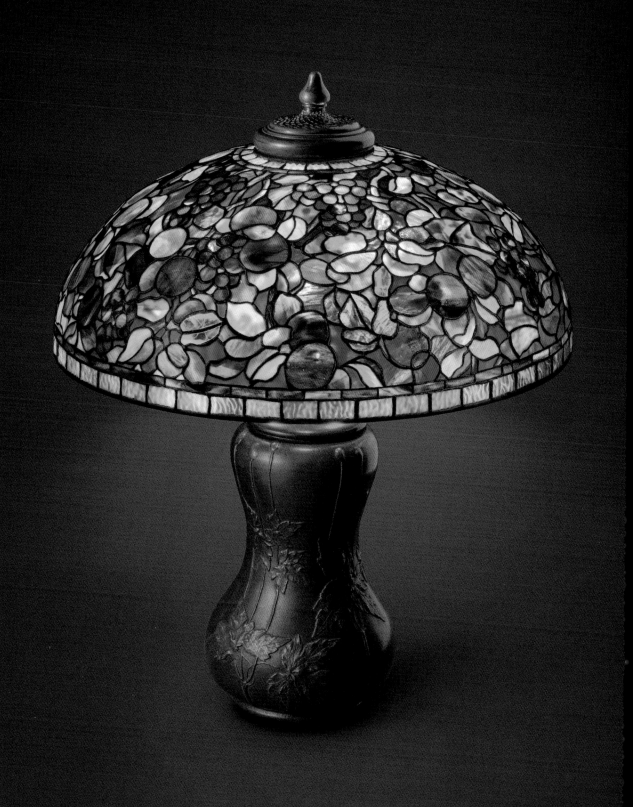

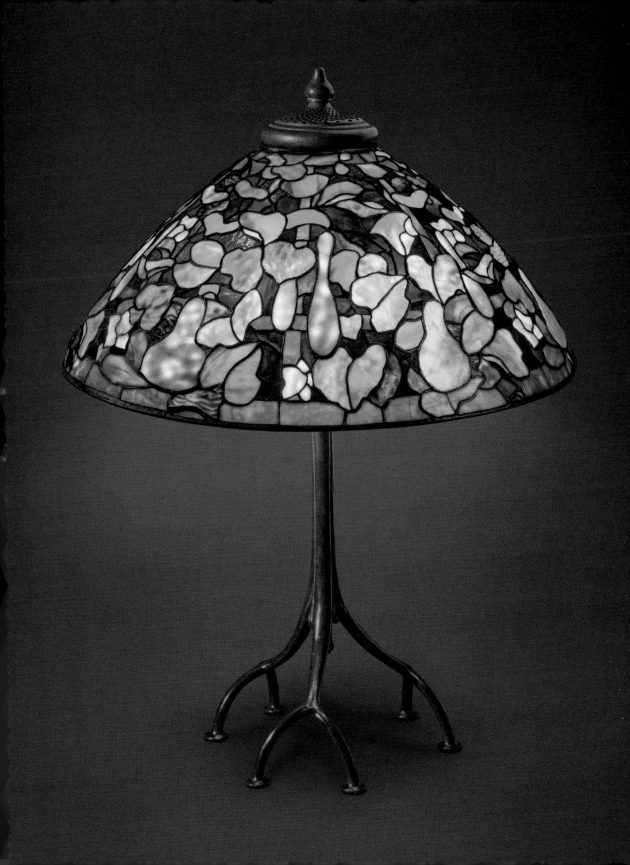

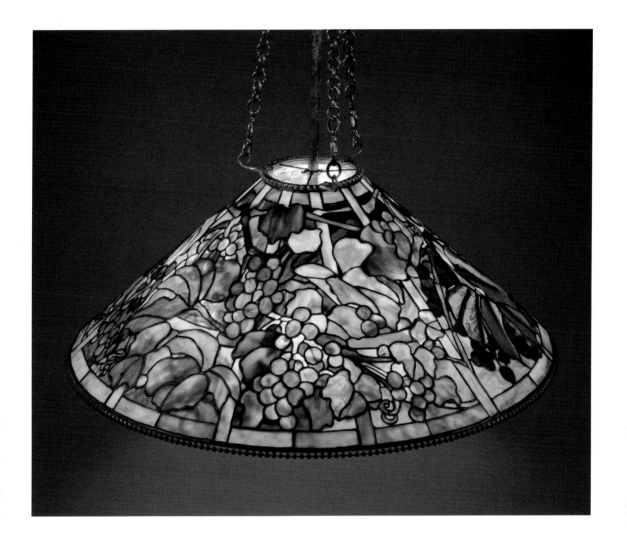

65 *GOURD* SHADE

Probably designed by Clara Driscoll ca. 1900–06

ROOT BASE

Designed ca. 1900–06

66 *GRAPE* HANGING SHADE

Probably designed by Clara Driscoll ca. 1900–06

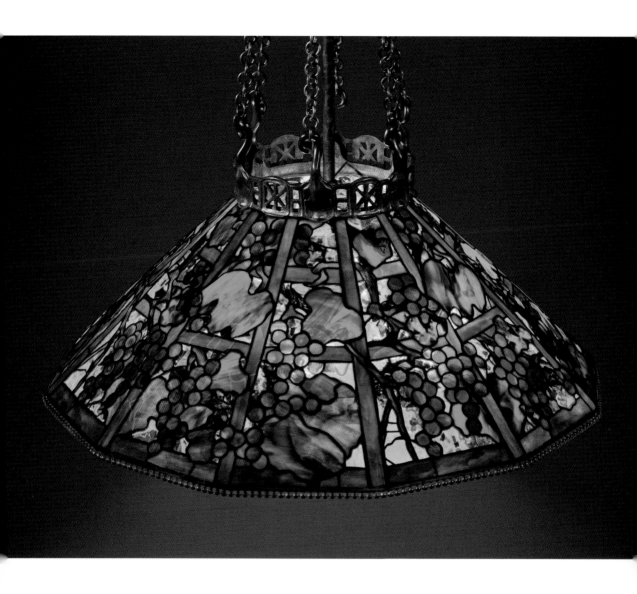

ABOVE

67 *GRAPE* HANGING SHADE

Probably designed by Clara Driscoll ca. 1900–06

OPPOSITE

68 *GRAPE* TABLE LAMP

Probably designed by Clara Driscoll ca. 1901–03

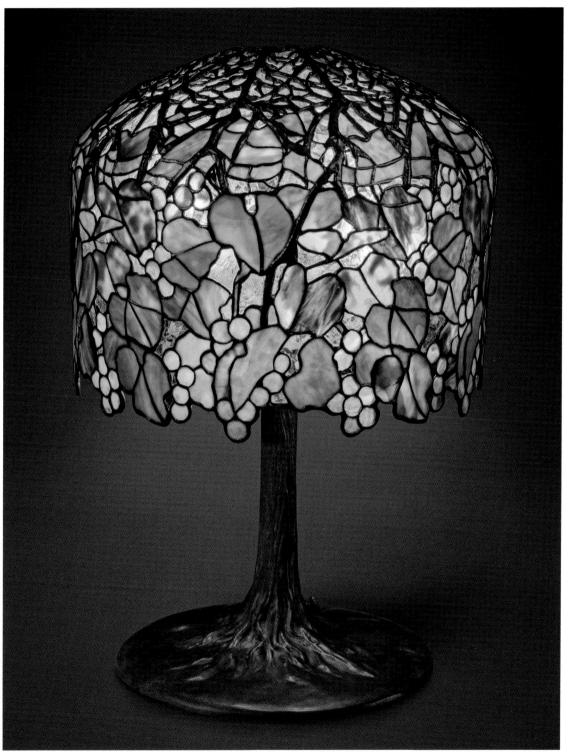

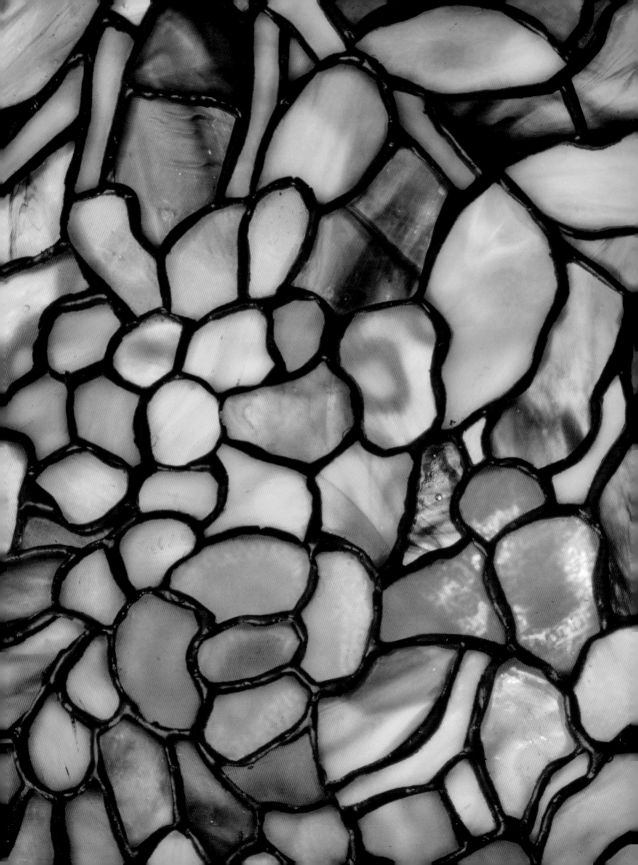

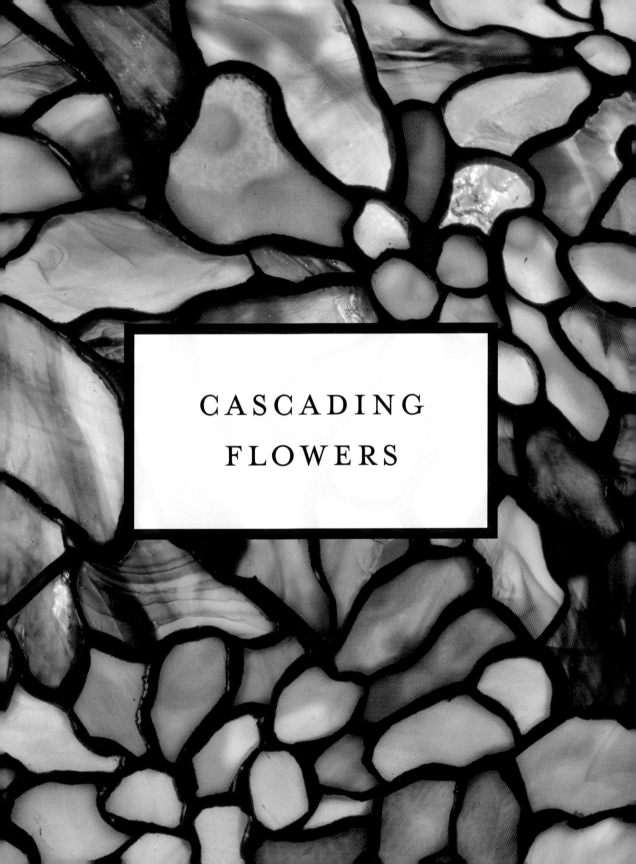

CASCADING
FLOWERS

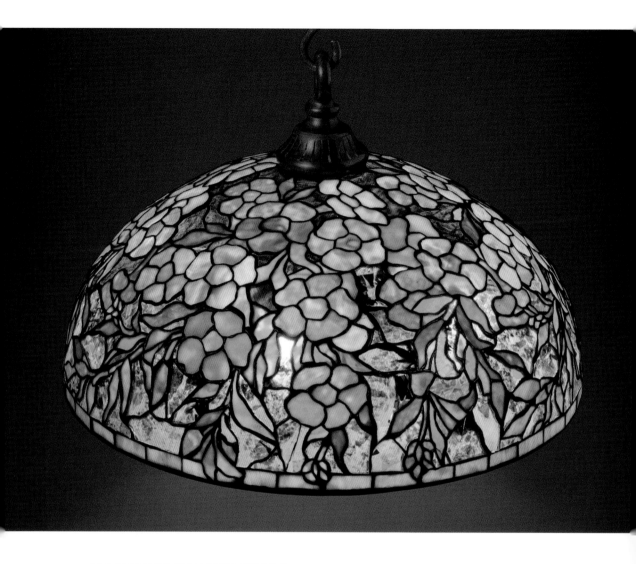

69 *ALLAMANDA* HANGING SHADE

Probably designed by Clara Driscoll ca. 1900–06

PRECEDING PAGES
Detail of lamp 73

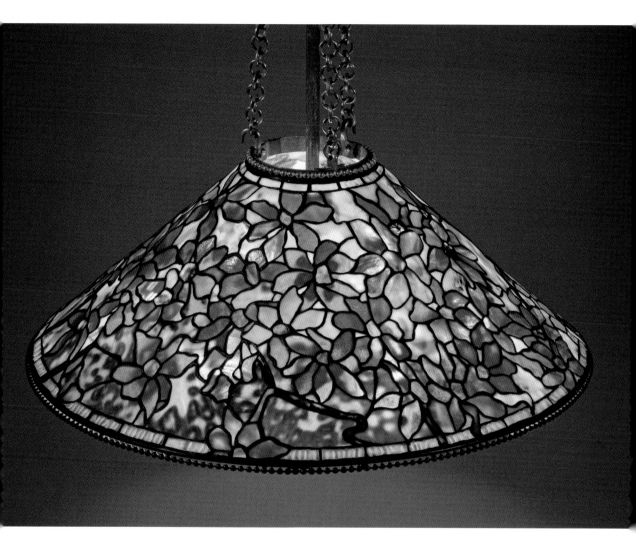

70 *CLEMATIS* HANGING SHADE

Probably designed by Clara Driscoll ca. 1900–06

Aficionados of the wild garden, which emerged in the 1870s, enjoyed the overgrown, unkempt qualities of climbing and creeping vines. As opposed to Victorian carpet beds laid out in geometric schemes, vines formed their own free-flowing blankets. Spreading unchecked over walls, climbers gave houses a desirable patina of age, and the sense that nature pervades all. Few flowers are naturally a true blue, and gardeners covet those that are. The shade depicts clematis flowers in transcendent shades from azure to cobalt and ultramarine.

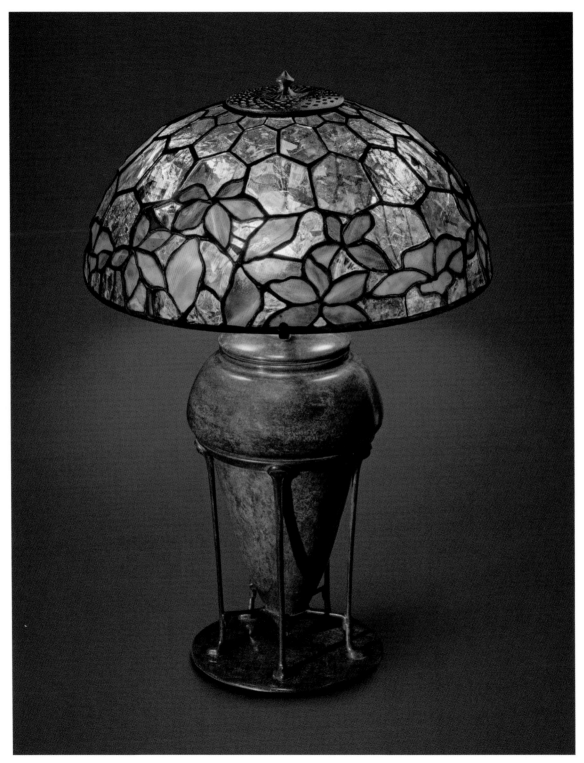

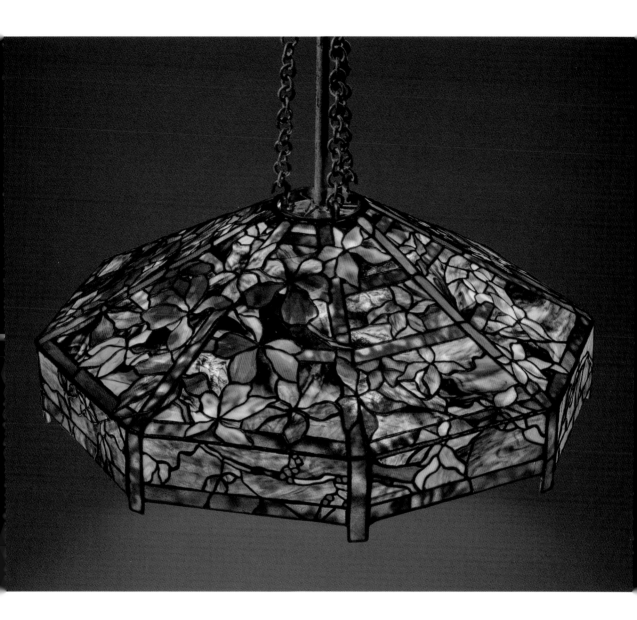

OPPOSITE

71 *WOODBINE* SHADE

Probably designed by Clara Driscoll ca. 1900–06

SPUN TORPEDO CRADLE BASE

Designed ca. 1900–02

ABOVE

72 *WOODBINE* HANGING SHADE

Probably designed by Clara Driscoll ca. 1900–06

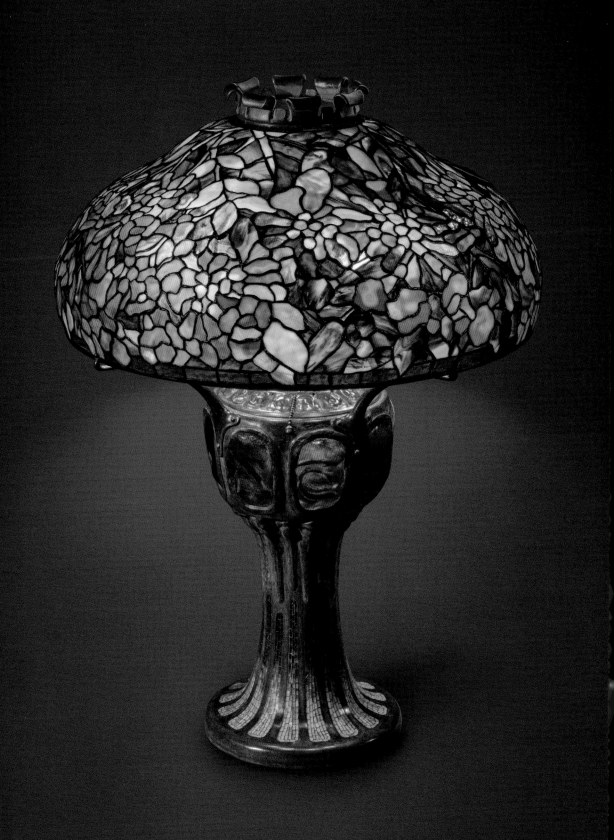

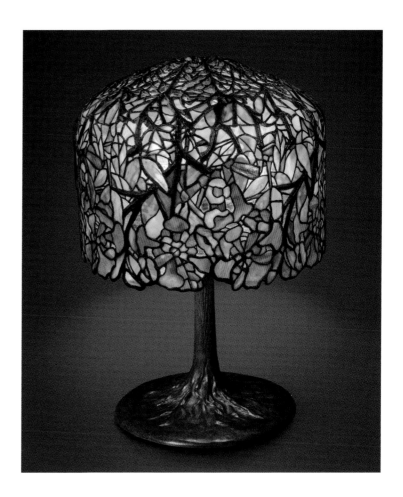

OPPOSITE

73 *TRUMPET CREEPER* SHADE

Probably designed by Clara Driscoll ca. 1900—06

ABOVE

74 *TRUMPET CREEPER* TABLE LAMP

Probably designed by Clara Driscoll ca. 1901—03

MOSAIC AND TURTLEBACK TILE BASE

Designed ca. 1900—02

For Louis C. Tiffany, color reigned over line and form. In a published lecture to a Brooklyn audience in 1917, he said, "Color is of the first importance. In many flowers their form is distinctly a secondary consideration, which comes after the satisfaction we feel in their colors—those hues that glow and flicker and strike like the embers, the many-colored jets and the steadier flames of a drift-wood fire." A comparable philosophy is at work in the dynamic *Trumpet Creeper* shade, where contrasts of textures and colors take precedence over botanical distinctions. The base features graduated stripes of mosaic inlay and large inset turtleback tiles.

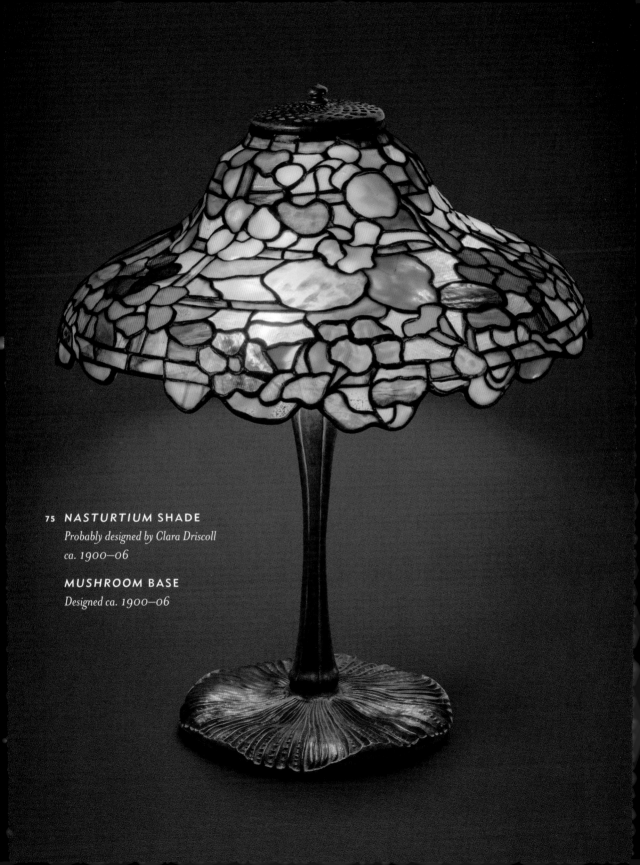

75 NASTURTIUM SHADE

Probably designed by Clara Driscoll
ca. 1900–06

MUSHROOM BASE

Designed ca. 1900–06

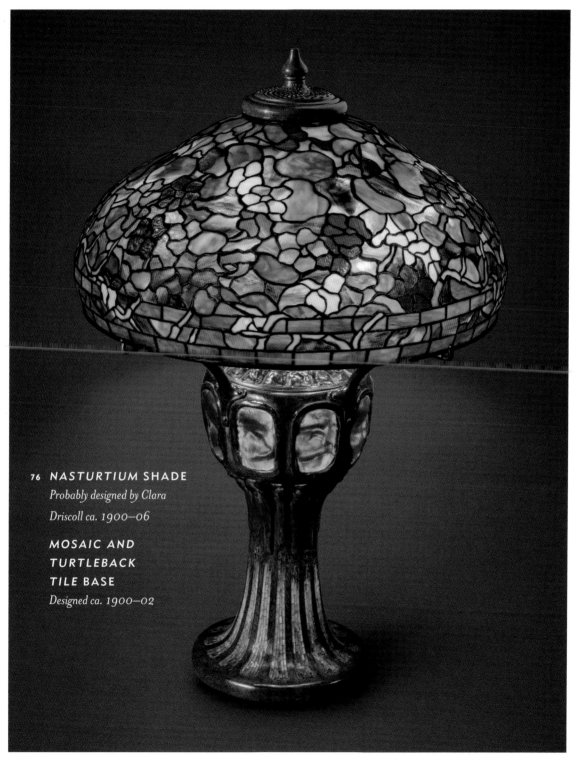

76 NASTURTIUM SHADE
Probably designed by Clara Driscoll ca. 1900–06

MOSAIC AND TURTLEBACK TILE BASE
Designed ca. 1900–02

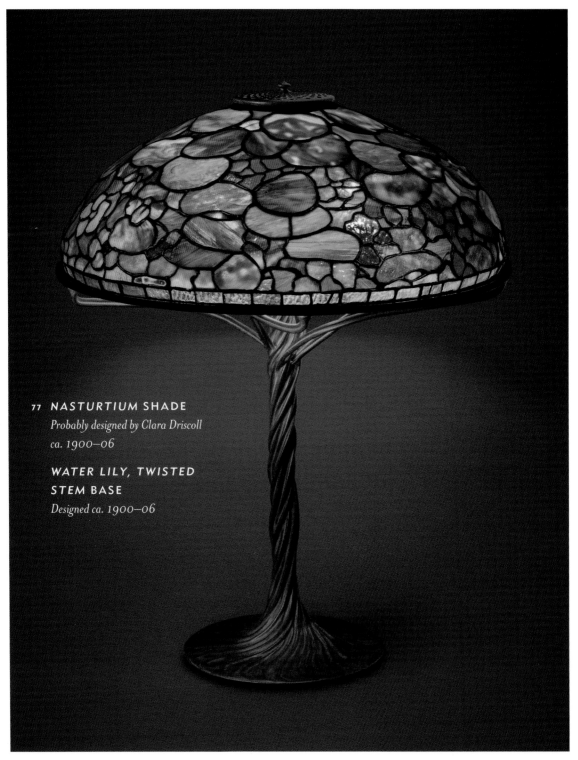

77 NASTURTIUM SHADE

Probably designed by Clara Driscoll
ca. 1900–06

WATER LILY, TWISTED STEM BASE

Designed ca. 1900–06

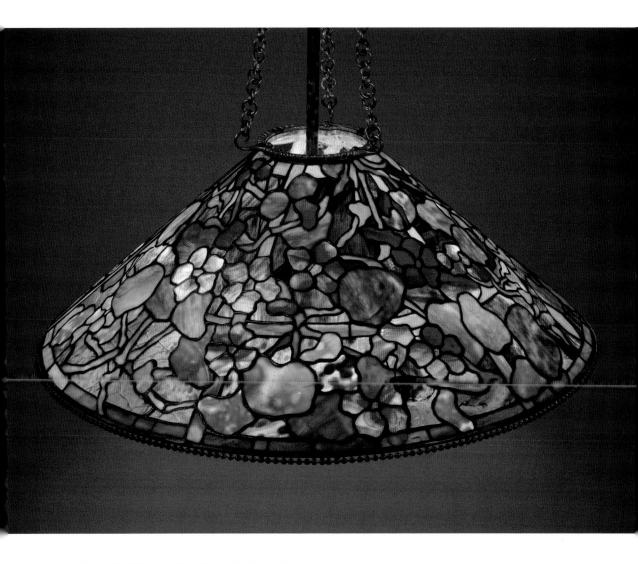

78 *NASTURTIUM* HANGING SHADE

Probably designed by Clara Driscoll ca. 1900—06

Describing the grounds at Laurelton Hall, Samuel Howe wrote in 1906, "There
is a little golden-colored creeper which defies all rules of etiquette and order
by running riot over walks, walls and beds, wreathing them in a sea of color,
gorgeous and sunny." Nasturtiums have a reputation for overtaking and crowding
out any other flower, and they will clamber with aplomb over trellises, as they
do in the *Nasturtium* hanging shade. "Yet who would check them, the truants,"
continued Howe. "What harmonizers! What decorative artists!"

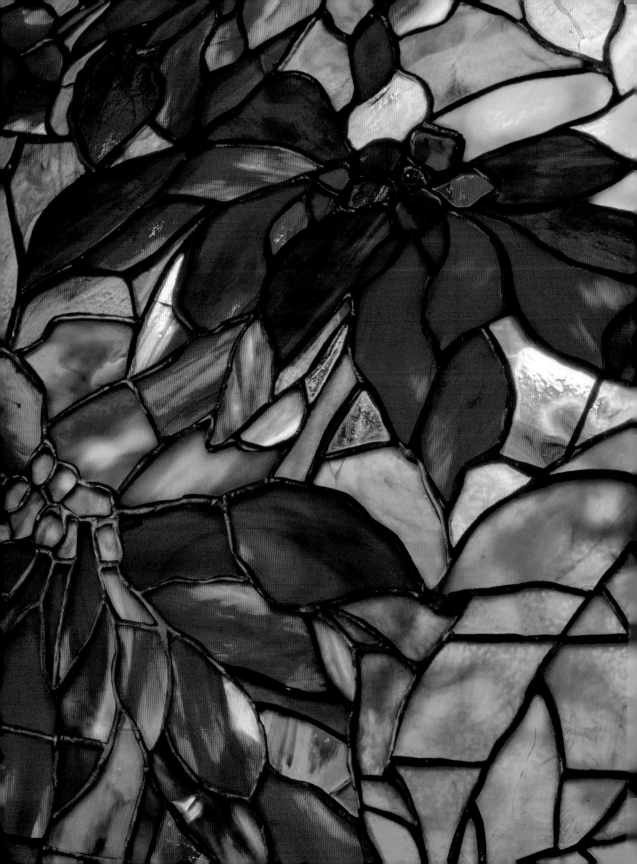

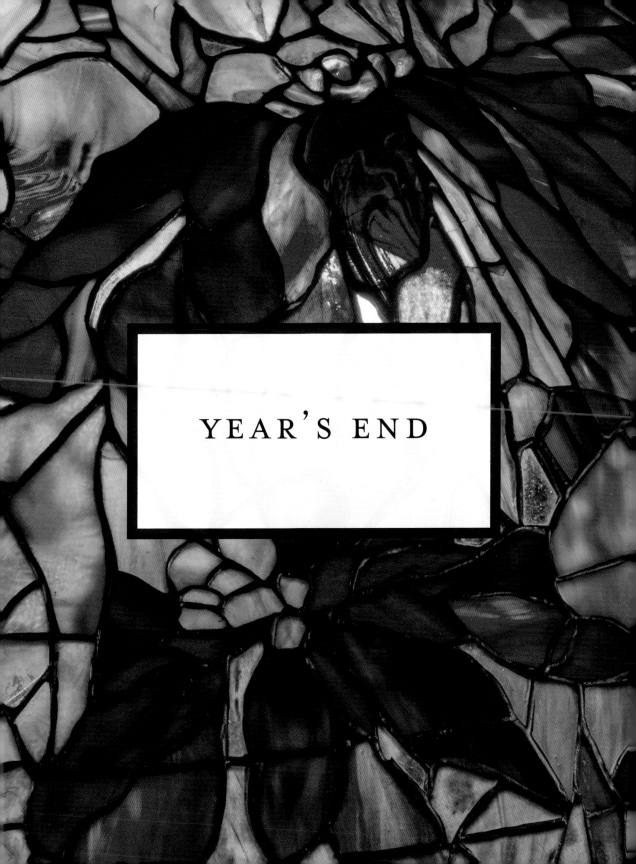

YEAR'S END

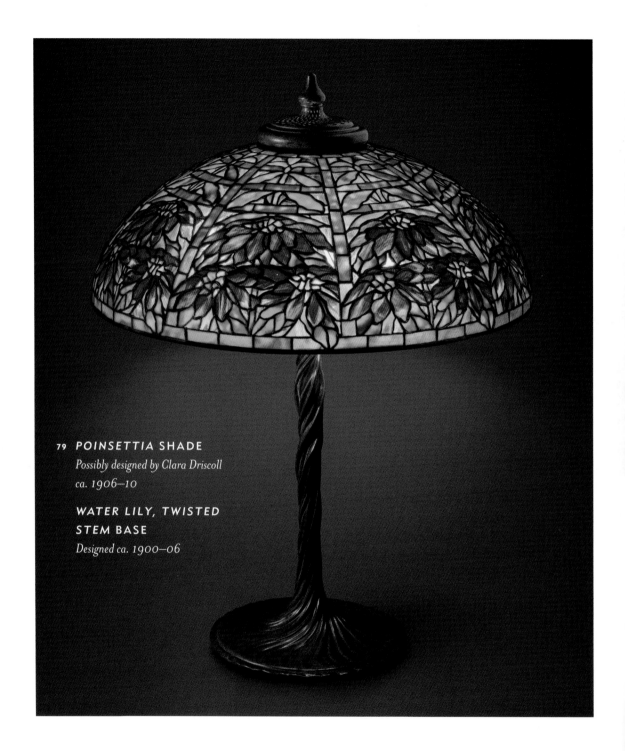

79 POINSETTIA SHADE
Possibly designed by Clara Driscoll
ca. 1906–10

**WATER LILY, TWISTED
STEM BASE**
Designed ca. 1900–06

PRECEDING PAGES
Detail of lamp 80

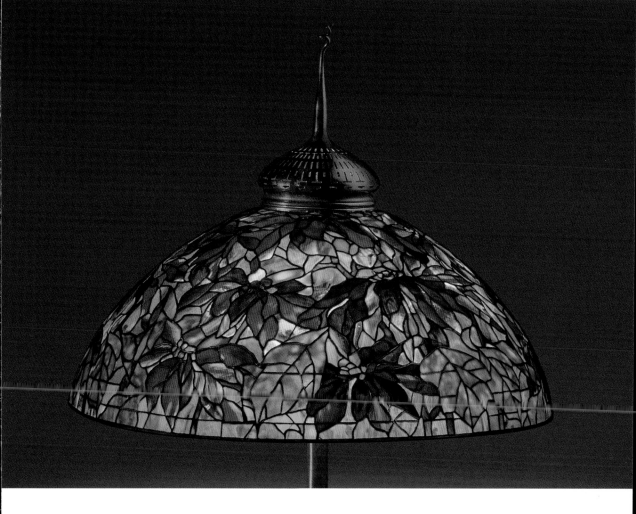

80 *POINSETTIA* SHADE

Possibly designed by Clara Driscoll ca. 1906—10

FLOOR BASE

Designed ca. 1910—13

Joel Roberts Poinsett, an amateur botanist and the first U.S. ambassador to a newly independent
Mexico, encountered a shrub with flaming red, flowerlike leaves near Taxco. It was known locally
as the "flor de Noche Buena," or Christmas Eve flower. Poinsett took cuttings to his home state
of South Carolina in 1828 and then distributed their descendants to horticulturalist friends and
botanical gardens. In the United States, the plants are associated with holiday interiors because
their bright bracts appear from October into January. A Tiffany Studios advertisement placed
in the *New York Times* in December 1908 declared that a *Poinsettia* hanging shade model, stylistically
similar to this floor lamp shade version, "possesses a distinctive Christmas atmosphere. [It] gives
the rich reds and greens of the Poinsettia with remarkable fidelity."

LIST OF ILLUSTRATED LAMPS

Names of lamps, shades, and bases derive from the Tiffany Studios *Price Lists* of 1906, 1910, and 1913. Dimensions are given as overall height by largest diameter or width. Hanging shade heights do not include hardware.

INSPIRED BY THE EAST

1 **HURRICANE LAMP**
Designed ca. 1894–96
25½ × 13 IN. (64.8 × 33 CM)
N84.1

2 **MOORISH CHANDELIER WITH FAVRILE SHADES**
Designed ca. 1900
MARKS ON SHADES: "L.C.T"
ON EACH
18 × 13 IN. (45.7 × 33 CM)
N84.6

3 **STALACTITE HANGING SHADE**
Designed ca. 1904–10
10½ × 8½ IN. (26.7 × 21.6 CM)
N84.10

4 **LOTUS, PAGODA SHADE**
Designed ca. 1900–04
MARKS: "TIFFANY STUDIOS"
AND "NEW YORK"
MUSHROOM BASE
Designed ca. 1900–02
MARKS: TIFFANY GLASS &
DECORATING CO. LOGO
AND "TIFFANY STUDIOS /
NEW YORK / 28622"
22 × 25 IN. (55.9 × 64.8 CM)
N84.21.1; NEUSTADT
COLLECTION OF TIFFANY GLASS,
N86.8.21

5 **BELL LAMP AND LOTUS SHADE**
Designed ca. 1900–06
MARK ON SHADE: "NEW YORK
TIFFANY STUDIOS"; BASE:
"TIFFANY STUDIOS / NEW

YORK / 6875"
21¼ × 16½ IN. (54 × 41.9 CM)
N84.32

6 **FAVRILE SHADES WITH PINEAPPLE BASE**
Designed ca. 1900–06
MARKS ON SHADES: "L.C.T."
ON EACH
31 × 29 IN. (78.7 × 73.7 CM)
N84.7

7 **GENTIAN SHADE**
Designed ca. 1900–06
MARK: "TIFFANY STUDIOS
NEW YORK"
INDIAN HOOKAH BASE
Designed ca. 1900–06
23 × 18 IN. (58.4 × 45.7 CM)
N84.29

8 **PEACOCK SHADE**
Probably designed by Clara Driscoll
ca. 1900–06
MARKS: "TIFFANY STUDIOS /
NEW YORK" AND "8663"
PEACOCK BASE
Designed ca. 1900–06
27½ × 18½ IN. (69.9 × 47 CM)
N84.86

ROMANTICIZING THE PAST

9 **COLONIAL SHADE**
Designed ca. 1906–10
MARK: "TIFFANY STUDIOS
NEW YORK 1564"
ROMAN BASE
Designed ca. 1906–10
MARK: "TIFFANY STUDIOS /
NEW YORK / 529"
30 × 25 IN. (76.2 × 63.5 CM)
N84.25.1, N84.89.2

10 **ELIZABETHAN SHADE**
Designed ca. 1910–13
MARK: "TIFFANY STUDIOS.
N.Y. 1954"

CLAW FEET LIBRARY BASE
Designed ca. 1900–06
MARK: "TIFFANY STVDIOS /
NEW YORK / 478"
25 × 23 IN. (63.5 × 58.4 CM)
N84.31

11 **EMPIRE SHADE**
Designed ca. 1910–13
MARK: "TIFFANY STVDIOS N.Y.
1953"
FIFTEENTH CENTURY BASE
Designed ca. 1906–10
MARK: "TIFFANY STUDIOS /
NEW YORK / 528"
26½ × 22½ IN. (67.3 × 57.2 CM)
N84.33.1, N84.83.2

12 **BOOKMARK SHADE**
Designed ca. 1906–10
MARK: "TIFFANY STUDIOS
NEW YORK"
CHASED POD FLOOR BASE
Designed ca. 1900–06
MARK: "TIFFANY STUDIOS /
NEW YORK / 376"
77 × 26 IN. (195.6 × 66 CM)
N84.36

13 **VENETIAN DESK LAMP**
Designed ca. 1906–08
MARK ON SHADE: "TIFFANY
STUDIOS NEW YORK 515";
BASE: "TIFFANY STUDIOS /
NEW YORK / 515"
20 × 13 IN. (50.8 × 33 CM)
N84.28

AT POND'S EDGE

14 **POND LILY SHADE**
Possibly designed by Clara Driscoll
ca. 1900–06
MARK: "TIFFANY STUDIOS NEW
YORK"
BLOWN GLASS IN METAL BASE
Designed ca. 1898–1900

MARK: "TIFFANY STUDIOS / NEW YORK"
24¼ × 20½ IN. (61.6 × 52.1 CM)
N84.50

15 SEAL LAMP WITH TURTLEBACK TILES
Designed ca. 1900–04
MARK: "TIFFANY STUDIOS / NEW YORK / 408 / 9948"
14½ × 8½ IN. (36.8 × 21.6 CM)
N84.22

16 ARROWHEAD SHADE
Probably designed by Clara Driscoll
ca. 1904
MARK: "TIFFANY STUDIOS / NEW YORK"
CATTAIL, POND LILY BASE
Designed ca. 1900–04
MARK: "TIFFANY STUDIOS / NEW YORK / 278"
25½ × 20½ IN. (64.8 × 52.1 CM)
N84.57

17 BAMBOO SHADE
Possibly designed by Clara Driscoll
ca. 1900–06
MARK: "TIFFANY STUDIOS NEW YORK 1443"
BAMBOO BASE
Designed ca. 1900–06
MARK: "TIFFANY STUDIOS / NEW YORK / 8097"
23 × 16 IN. (58.4 × 40.6 CM)
N84.78

18 BAMBOO SHADE
Possibly designed by Clara Driscoll
ca. 1900–06
MARK: "TIFFANY STUDIOS NEW YORK 1521–2"
BAMBOO FLOOR BASE
Designed ca. 1900–06
67 × 24 IN. (170.2 × 61 CM)
N84.85

DRAGONFLIES AND POPPIES

19 DRAGONFLY SHADE
Probably designed by Clara Driscoll
ca. 1900–06
MARKS: "TIFFANY STUDIOS NEW YORK" AND "1507"
STANDARD BASE WITH FAVRILE GLASS BALLS
Designed ca. 1900–03
MARK: "TIFFANY STUDIOS / NEW YORK / 10918"
28½ × 22 IN. (72.4 × 55.9 CM)
N84.113

20 DRAGONFLY SHADE
Probably designed by Clara Driscoll
ca. 1900–06
MARK: "TIFFANY STUDIOS / NEW YORK"
SPUN OVAL BASE WITH THREE-LEAF TURTLEBACK TILE ORNAMENT
Designed ca. 1900–06
MARKS: "TIFFANY STUDIOS / NEW YORK." AND TIFFANY STUDIOS MONOGRAM
22½ × 16¾ IN. (57.2 × 42.5 CM)
N84.52

21 DRAGONFLY SHADE
Probably designed by Clara Driscoll
ca. 1900–06
MARKS: "TIFFANY STUDIOS / NEW YORK" AND "1507–29"
STANDARD BASE WITH FAVRILE GLASS BALLS
Designed ca. 1900–03
MARKS: "TIFFANY STUDIOS / NEW YORK" AND "10922"
31½ × 22 IN. (80 × 55.9 CM)
N84.110

22 DRAGONFLY SHADE
Probably designed by Clara Driscoll
ca. 1900–06
MARK: "1495 TIFFANY STUDIOS NEW YORK"

WATER LILY, TWISTED STEM BASE
Designed ca. 1900–06
MARK: "TIFFANY STUDIOS. / NEW YORK / S220 / 443"
28½ × 21 IN. (72.4 × 53.3 CM)
N84.54

23 DRAGONFLY SHADE
Probably designed by Clara Driscoll
ca. 1900–06
HAMMERED CUSHION BASE
Designed ca. 1900–06
MARK: "TIFFANY STUDIOS / NEW YORK / 364"
27½ × 17 IN. (69.9 × 43.2 CM)
N84.67

24 POPPY SHADE
Probably designed by Clara Driscoll
ca. 1900–06
MARK: "TIFFANY STUDIOS / NEW YORK / 1461"
BLOWN GLASS IN METAL BASE
Designed ca. 1900–11
MARK: "TIFFANY STUDIOS / NEW YORK / [TIFFANY GLASS & DECORATING CO. LOGO] / 21667"
23 × 17 IN. (58.4 × 43.2 CM)
N84.66.1, N84.94.2

25 POPPY SHADE
Probably designed by Clara Driscoll
ca. 1900–06
MARK: "TIFFANY STUDIOS NEW YORK 1531"
WATER LILY, TWISTED STEM BASE
Designed ca. 1900–06
MARK: "TIFFANY STUDIOS. / NEW YORK / 443"
27½ × 20¼ IN. (69.9 × 51.4 CM)
N84.56

26 POPPY SHADE
Possibly designed by Clara Driscoll
ca. 1906–10
MARK: "TIFFANY STUDIOS NEW YORK 1597"

SCROLL FLOOR BASE

Designed ca. 1900–06

MARK: "TIFFANY STUDIOS / NEW
YORK / 375"

70½ × 26½ IN. (179.1 × 67.3 CM)

N84.107

27 *ORIENTAL POPPY* SHADE

Designed ca. 1910–13

MARK: "TIFFANY STUDIOS NEW
YORK 1902"

SCROLL FLOOR BASE

Designed ca. 1900–06

MARK: "TIFFANY STUDIOS / NEW
YORK / S185"

70½ × 26 IN. (179.1 × 66 CM)

N84.109

28 *POPPY* SHADE

*Probably designed by Clara Driscoll
ca. 1900–06*

MARK: "TIFFANY STUDIOS NEW
YORK [ILLEGIBLE]"

RIBBED CUSHION BASE

Designed ca. 1900–02

MARKS: TIFFANY GLASS &
DECORATING CO. LOGO, "D 794,"
AND "2"

21½ × 17 IN. (54.6 × 43.2 CM)

N84.55.1, N84.38.2

GARDEN PERENNIALS

29 *DAFFODIL* SHADE

*Probably designed by Clara Driscoll
ca. 1900–06*

MARK: "TIFFANY STUDIOS NEW
YORK 1497"

WATER LILY, TWISTED STEM
BASE

Designed ca. 1900–06

MARK: "TIFFANY STUDIOS / NEW
YORK / 443"

28 × 20 IN. (71.1 × 50.8 CM)

N84.62.1, N84.25.2

30 *DAFFODIL* SHADE

*Probably designed by Clara Driscoll
ca. 1900–06*

MARK: "TIFFANY STUDIOS NEW
YORK 2–1060"

CRUTCH OVAL BASE WITH
TURTLEBACK TILE BAND

Designed ca. 1900–06

MARKS: "TIFFANY STUDIOS / NEW
YORK / S228," "446," AND "8"

23 × 20 IN. (58.4 × 50.8 CM)

N84.64.1, N84.62.2

31 *DAFFODIL AND NARCISSUS*
SHADE

Designed ca. 1910–13

MARK: "TIFFANY STUDIOS NEW
YORK 1917"

CRUTCH OVAL BASE WITH
TURTLEBACK TILE BAND

Designed ca. 1900–06

26 × 20 IN. (66 × 50.8 CM)

N84.97

32 *DAFFODIL* HANGING SHADE

*Probably designed by Clara Driscoll
ca. 1900–06*

MARK: "TIFFANY STUDIOS NEW
YORK"

11½ × 28 IN. (29.2 × 71.1 CM)

N84.51

33 *DAFFODIL* SHADE

*Probably designed by Clara Driscoll
ca. 1900–06*

MUD TURTLE CUSHION BASE

Designed ca. 1900–06

MARK: "TIFFANY STUDIOS. / NEW
YORK"

21½ × 16 IN. (54.6 × 40.6 CM)

N84.81

34 *TULIP* SHADE

*Possibly designed by Clara Driscoll
ca. 1906–10*

MARK: "TIFFANY STUDIOS NEW
YORK 1548"

ARCH AND LEAF BASE

Designed ca. 1910–13

MARKS: "TIFFANY STUDIOS / NEW
YORK" AND "542"

29½ × 22 IN. (74.9 × 55.9 CM)

N84.92

35 *DAFFODIL* SHADE

Designed ca. 1910–13

MARK: "TIFFANY STUDIOS NEW
YORK 1919"

STANDARD BASE WITH
FAVRILE GLASS BALLS

Designed ca. 1900–06

MARKS: "TIFFANY STUDIOS / NEW
YORK" AND "399 A"

31 × 21 IN. (78.7 × 53.3 CM)

N84.90.1, N84.65.2

36 *TULIP* SHADE

*Possibly designed by Clara Driscoll
ca. 1906–10*

MARK: "TIFFANY STUDIOS NEW
YORK"

POD CUSHION BASE

Designed ca. 1900–03

MARKS: "TIFFANY STUDIOS / NEW
YORK" AND "307"

31½ × 24½ IN. (80 × 62.2 CM)

N84.89.1, N84.105.2

SIGNS OF SPRING

37 *DOGWOOD* SHADE

*Probably designed by Clara Driscoll
ca. 1900–06*

MARK: "TIFFANY STUDIOS / NEW
YORK"

CHASED POD FLOOR BASE

Designed ca. 1900–06

MARK: "TIFFANY STUDIOS / NEW
YORK / 376"

74 × 25 IN. (188 × 63.5 CM)

N84.114.1, 2015.18

38 *DOGWOOD* HANGING SHADE

*Probably designed by Clara Driscoll
ca. 1900–06*

MARK: "TIFFANY STUDIOS
NEW YORK"

10 × 29 IN. (25.4 × 73.7 CM)

N84.71

39 *DOGWOOD* SHADE

*Probably designed by Clara Driscoll
ca. 1900–06*

MARK: "TIFFANY STUDIOS NEW
YORK"

PIANO FLOOR BASE
Designed ca. 1900–06
MARK: "TIFFANY STUDIOS / NEW
YORK / 9942"
63½ × 22 IN. (161.3 × 55.9 CM)
N84.48

40 *MAGNOLIA* SHADE
*Possibly designed by Clara Driscoll
ca. 1906–10*
MARK: "TIFFANY STUDIOS NEW
YORK 1599"
CHASED POD FLOOR BASE
Designed ca. 1900–06
MARK: "TIFFANY STUDIOS /
NEW YORK / 376"
78 × 28 IN. (198.1 × 71.1 CM)
N84.108

41 *SNOWBALL* SHADE
*Probably designed by Clara Driscoll
ca. 1900–06*
MARK: "TIFFANY STUDIOS NEW
YORK"
FLOOR BASE
Designed ca. 1900–06
14 × 25 IN. (35.6 × 63.5 CM)
N84.119

42 *SNOWBALL* HANGING SHADE
*Probably designed by Clara Driscoll
ca. 1900–06*
MARK: "TIFFANY STUDIOS /
NEW YORK"
12 × 28 IN. (30.5 × 71.1 CM)
N84.72.1

BLOSSOMING CANOPIES

43 *WISTERIA* TABLE LAMP
Designed by Clara Driscoll ca. 1901
MARK ON SHADE: "7806";
BASE: "7806 / TIFFANY STUDIOS /
NEW YORK."
27½ × 18½ IN. (69.9 × 47 CM)
N84.130

44 *WISTERIA* TABLE LAMP
Designed by Clara Driscoll ca. 1901
MARKS ON SHADE: "TIFFANY
STVDIOS N[EW YORK]"; BASE:

[TIFFANY GLASS & DECORATING
CO. LOGO] / "TIFFANY STUDIOS /
NEW YORK" AND "26854"
27 × 18 IN. (68.6 × 45.7 CM)
N84.127

45 *LABURNUM* SHADE
*Probably designed by Clara Driscoll
ca. 1901–06*
MARK: "TIFFANY STUDIOS /
NEW YORK"
SCROLL FLOOR BASE
Designed ca. 1900–06
MARK: "TIFFANY STUDIOS /
NEW YORK / 3118"
79 × 28 IN. (200.7 × 71.1 CM)
N84.123

46 *LABURNUM* SHADE
*Probably designed by Clara Driscoll
ca. 1901–06*
MARK: "TIFFANY STUDIOS /
NEW YORK 1539"
BIRD SKELETON BASE
Designed ca. 1900–06
MARKS: "TIFFANY STUDIOS /
NEW YORK" AND "442"
29 × 22 IN. (73.7 × 55.9 CM)
N84.116

47 *APPLE BLOSSOM* TABLE LAMP
*Probably designed by Clara Driscoll
ca. 1901–06*
MARK ON SHADE: "TIFFANY
STUDIOS NEW YORK"; BASE:
"TIFFANY STUDIOS / NEW
YORK / 351"
29 × 25¼ IN. (73.7 × 64.1 CM)
N84.124

48 *APPLE BLOSSOM* TABLE LAMP
*Probably designed by Clara Driscoll
ca. 1901–06*
MARKS ON SHADE: "8021"; BASE:
"TIFFANY STUDIOS / NEW YORK. /
7879" AND "346"
27½ × 18 IN. (69.9 × 45.7 CM)
N84.129

49 *PONY APPLE BLOSSOM*
TABLE LAMP

*Probably designed by Clara Driscoll
ca. 1901–06*
MARK ON SHADE: "TIFFANY
STUDIOS / NEW YORK / 384–5"
17½ × 10½ IN. (44.5 × 26.7 CM)
N84.125

50 *APPLE BLOSSOM* HANGING
SHADE
Designed ca. 1910
MARK: "TIFFANY STUDIOS NEW
YORK"
12 × 24¼ IN. (30.5 × 61.6 CM)
N84.101

51 *COBWEB* SHADE, *MOSAIC
FLORAL* BASE
Designed by Clara Driscoll ca. 1902
28½ × 22 IN. (72.4 × 55.9 CM)
N84.128

THE COTTAGE GARDEN

52 *CYCLAMEN* SHADE
*Probably designed by Clara Driscoll
ca. 1900–06*
LEAF CUSHION BASE
Designed ca. 1900–02
MARKS: TIFFANY GLASS &
DECORATING CO. LOGO
AND "TIFFANY STUDIOS / NEW
YORK / 28618"
22½ × 16 IN. (57.2 × 40.6 CM)
N84.63.1, N84.45.2

53 *PANSY* SHADE
*Probably designed by Clara Driscoll
ca. 1900–06*
NIGHT BLOOMING CEREUS
BASE
Designed ca. 1900–02
MARKS: "TIFFANY STUDIOS /
NEW YORK / 27477" AND TIFFANY
GLASS & DECORATING CO. LOGO
13 × 16 IN. (33 × 40.6 CM)
N84.44

54 *BLACK-EYED SUSAN* SHADE
*Probably designed by Clara Driscoll
ca. 1900–06*
MARK: "TIFFANY STUDIOS

NEW YORK"
SPUN OVAL BASE WITH
THREE-LEAF TURTLEBACK
TILE ORNAMENT
Designed ca. 1900—06
MARK: TIFFANY STUDIOS
MONOGRAM
17 × 16 IN. (43.2 × 40.6 CM)
N84.39.1, N84.80.2

55 *ROSE* SHADE
Probably designed by Clara Driscoll
ca. 1900—06
CONVENTIONAL CUSHION BASE
Designed ca. 1900—06
MARK: "TIFFANY STUDIOS /
NEW YORK. / 26874"
23¾ × 16½ IN. (57.8 × 41.9 CM)
N84.58.1, N84.16.2

56 *ROSE* SHADE
Designed ca. 1910—13
MARK: "TIFFANY STUDIOS NEW
YORK 1915"
ROMAN BASE
Designed ca. 1906—10
MARK: "TIFFANY STUDIOS / NEW
YORK / 529"
27½ × 25 IN. (69.9 × 63.4 CM)
N84.98.1, N84.101.2

57 *HOLLYHOCK* HANGING SHADE
Probably designed by Clara Driscoll
ca. 1900—06
MARK: "TIFFANY STUDIOS
NEW YORK 625—1"
12 × 28 IN. (30.5 × 71.1 CM)
N84.77

58 *PEONY BORDER* SHADE
Possibly designed by Clara Driscoll
ca. 1906—10
MARK: "TIFFANY STUDIOS NEW
YORK 1574"
CHASED POD FLOOR BASE
Designed ca. 1900—06
MARK: "TIFFANY STUDIOS /
NEW YORK / 376"
73 × 24½ IN. (185.4 × 62.2 CM)
N84.47

59 *PEONY* HANGING SHADE
Probably designed by Clara Driscoll
ca. 1900—04
MARK: "TIFFANY STUDIOS NEW
YORK"
12 × 28½ IN. (30.5 × 72.4 CM)
N84.76

60 *PEONY* SHADE
Probably designed by Clara Driscoll
ca. 1900—04
MARK: "TIFFANY STUDIOS NEW
YORK 1505"
CUSHION BASE
Designed ca. 1900—06
31½ × 22 IN. (80 × 55.9 CM)
N84.105.1, N84.112.2

61 *PEONY* SHADE
Probably designed by Clara Driscoll
ca. 1900—04
MARK: "TIFFANY STUDIOS
NEW YORK"
TEAR CUSHION BASE
Designed ca. 1900—06
MARKS: "TIFFANY STUDIOS. /
NEW YORK / 359" AND "S173"
23 × 18½ IN. (58.4 × 47 CM)
N84.83.1, N84.88.2

62 *PEONY* SHADE
Probably designed by Clara Driscoll
ca. 1900—04
MARK: "TIFFANY STUDIOS NEW
YORK 1509"
LIBRARY STANDARD BASE
Designed ca. 1900—06
MARK: "TIFFANY STUDIOS / NEW
YORK / 397"
28½ × 22 IN. (72.4 × 55.9 CM)
N84.87

63 *PEONY* HANGING SHADE
Probably designed by Clara Driscoll
ca. 1900—04
MARK: "TIFFANY STUDIOS NEW
YORK"
12 × 29 IN. (30.5 × 73.7 CM)
N84.75

FRUITFUL VINES

64 *FRUIT* SHADE
Probably designed by Clara Driscoll
ca. 1900—06
MARK: "TIFFANY STUDIOS
NEW YORK 1519"
BRONZE POTTERY BASE
Designed ca. 1908
MARK: "L.C. TIFFANY FAVRILE
BRONZE POTTERY"
31 × 24 IN. (78.7 × 61 CM)
N84.104

65 *GOURD* SHADE
Probably designed by Clara Driscoll
ca. 1900—06
MARK: "TIFFANY STUDIOS NEW
YORK 1522—1"
ROOT BASE
Designed ca. 1900—06
34½ × 24½ IN. (87.6 × 62.2 CM)
N84.102

66 *GRAPE* HANGING SHADE
Probably designed by Clara Driscoll
ca. 1900—06
MARK: "TIFFANY STUDIOS / NEW
YORK / 608—10"
12 × 28 IN. (30.5 × 71.1 CM)
N84.73

67 *GRAPE* HANGING SHADE
Probably designed by Clara Driscoll
ca. 1900—06
MARK: "TIFFANY STUDIOS
NEW YORK"
12½ × 30 IN. (31.8 × 76.2 CM)
N84.60

68 *GRAPE* TABLE LAMP
Probably designed by Clara Driscoll
ca. 1901—03
MARKS ON SHADE: "TIFFANY
STUDIOS / NEW YORK/ 348—3"
AND "11016"; BASE: "TIFFANY
STUDIOS / NEW YORK/ 342" AND
"S1320"
27½ × 18 IN. (69.9 × 45.7 CM)
N84.126

CASCADING FLOWERS

69 *ALLAMANDA* HANGING SHADE
Probably designed by Clara Driscoll
ca. 1900–06
MARK: "TIFFANY STUDIOS
NEW YORK"
13 × 20 IN. (33 × 50.8 CM)
N84.100

70 *CLEMATIS* HANGING SHADE
Probably designed by Clara Driscoll
ca. 1900–06
MARK: "TIFFANY STUDIOS /
NEW YORK"
9¼ × 24 IN. (23.5 × 61 CM)
N84.70

71 *WOODBINE* SHADE
Probably designed by Clara Driscoll
ca. 1900–06
MARK: "TIFFANY STUDIOS
NEW YORK"
SPUN TORPEDO CRADLE BASE
Designed ca. 1900–02
MARK: "29939 / TIFFANY
STUDIOS / NEW YORK. /
[TIFFANY GLASS &
DECORATING CO. LOGO]"
21¼ × 14 IN. (54 × 35.6 CM)
N84.46

72 *WOODBINE* HANGING SHADE
Probably designed by Clara Driscoll
ca. 1900–06
MARKS: "TIFFANY STUDIOS
NEW YORK" AND "609-1"
10½ × 25 IN. (26.7 × 63.5 CM)
N84.111

73 *TRUMPET CREEPER* SHADE
Probably designed by Clara Driscoll
ca. 1900–06
MARK: "TIFFANY STUDIOS
NEW YORK"
*MOSAIC AND TURTLEBACK
TILE* BASE
Designed ca. 1900–02
MARK: "TIFFANY STUDIOS /
NEW YORK / [TIFFANY GLASS &

DECORATING CO. LOGO] / 2674"
28½ × 22 IN. (72.4 × 55.9 CM)
N84.99

74 *TRUMPET CREEPER* TABLE LAMP
Probably designed by Clara Driscoll
ca. 1901–03
MARKS ON SHADE: "1080"
AND "TIFFANY STUDIOS / NEW
YORK / 346–5"; BASE: "TIFFANY
STUDIOS / NEW YORK. / 10117"
29 × 18½ IN. (73.7 × 47 CM)
N84.131

75 *NASTURTIUM* SHADE
Probably designed by Clara Driscoll
ca. 1900–06
MARK: "TIFFANY STVDIOS
NEW YORK"
MUSHROOM BASE
Designed ca. 1900–06
MARKS: "TIFFANY STUDIOS. /
NEW YORK / 337" AND "S231"
19½ × 16 IN. (49.5 × 40.6 CM)
N84.118

76 *NASTURTIUM* SHADE
Probably designed by Clara Driscoll
ca. 1900–06
MARK: "TIFFANY STUDIOS NEW
YORK 1506-2"
*MOSAIC AND TURTLEBACK
TILE* BASE
Designed ca. 1900–02
MARK: "TIFFANY STUDIOS /
NEW YORK."
34½ × 23 IN. (87.6 × 58.4 CM)
N84.106

77 *NASTURTIUM* SHADE
Probably designed by Clara Driscoll
ca. 1900–06
MARK: "TIFFANY STUDIOS NEW
YORK"
WATER LILY, TWISTED STEM
BASE
Designed ca. 1900–06
MARK: "TIFFANY STUDIOS /
NEW YORK / S230"
27½ × 20½ IN. (69.9 × 52.1 CM)
N84.93

78 *NASTURTIUM* HANGING SHADE
Probably designed by Clara Driscoll
ca. 1900–06
MARK: "TIFFANY STUDIOS
NEW YORK 602-3"
12 × 28 IN. (30.5 × 71.1 CM)
N84.74

YEAR'S END

79 *POINSETTIA* SHADE
Possibly designed by Clara Driscoll
ca. 1906–10
MARK: "TIFFANY STUDIOS NEW
YORK 1551"
WATER LILY, TWISTED STEM
BASE
Designed ca. 1900–06
MARK: "TIFFANY STUDIOS /
NEW YORK. / 443"
26 × 22 IN. (66 × 55.9 CM)
N84.103.1, N84.121.2

80 *POINSETTIA* SHADE
Possibly designed by Clara Driscoll
ca. 1906–10
MARK: "TIFFANY STUDIOS
NEW YORK 1528"
FLOOR BASE
Designed ca. 1910–13
MARK: "TIFFANY STUDIOS /
NEW YORK / 645"
78 × 26 IN. (198.1 × 66 CM)
N84.95

CHRONOLOGY

1848

FEBRUARY 18 Louis Comfort Tiffany (LCT) is born in New York City to Charles Lewis Tiffany (1812–1902) and Harriet Olivia Avery Young (1817–1897).

1861

DECEMBER 15 Clara Driscoll is born Clara Pierce Wolcott in Tallmadge, Ohio, to Elizur Wolcott (1833–1873) and Fannie L. Pierce (1834–1906).

1866

NOVEMBER 12 LCT begins art training at the National Academy of Design in New York City.

1868–69

LCT studies painting in Paris with Léon-Charles Adrien Bailly (1826–1871).

1870–71

LCT travels in Europe and North Africa with painter Robert Swain Gifford (1840–1905) and begins painting Orientalist scenes.

1875–77

LCT first experiments with glass at Thill's Empire State Flint Glass Works in Brooklyn.

1876

MAY–NOVEMBER LCT exhibits paintings and watercolors, primarily North African subjects, at the Centennial International Exhibition in Philadelphia.

1878

LCT opens his first glass house under the supervision of Venetian glassblower Andrea Boldini; it burns down twice and is rebuilt.

LCT produces his first ecclesiastical window, for St. Mark's Episcopal Church in Islip, New York.

1879

SUMMER LCT joins textile designer Candace T. Wheeler (1827–1923) in founding the interior decorating firm Tiffany & Wheeler (1879–81) at 335 Fourth Avenue in New York City.

NOVEMBER 4 Thomas A. Edison files patent for an incandescent light bulb.

1881

FEBRUARY 8 LCT receives patents for opalescent glass, two years after the first patent application by rival John La Farge (1835–1910).

MAY 8 LCT is elected an academician of the National Academy of Design.

JUNE 15 LCT forms the interior decorating firm of Louis C. Tiffany and Co., Associated Artists (1881–83) at 333–335 Fourth Avenue. Works with Candace Wheeler, artist Lockwood de Forest (1850–1932), and others.

1882

LCT decorates the Blue Room of the White House with gaslight wall sconces incorporating glass mosaic decoration and iridescent glass pendants.

1883

Louis C. Tiffany & Co., Associated Artists, becomes Louis C. Tiffany and Company.

1884

Wolcott completes design training at the Western Reserve School of Design for Women in Cleveland, Ohio.

1885

LCT decorates the Lyceum Theater in New York City with electric chandeliers and sconces, in collaboration with Thomas Edison.

DECEMBER 1 LCT forms Tiffany Glass Company (1885–92) at 333 Fourth Avenue, corner of Twenty-fifth Street.

1888

MARCH Wolcott studies industrial design at the Metropolitan Museum Art School, New York City.

JUNE She begins work at Tiffany Glass Company.

1889

LCT visits the glass atelier of Émile Gallé (1846–1904) in Nancy, France.

NOVEMBER 28 Wolcott leaves Tiffany Glass Company to marry Francis S. Driscoll.

1891

LCT constructs a six-story building at 102 East Twenty-fifth Street, adjacent to his building on Fourth Avenue, which eventually houses the Women's Glass Cutting Department (fig. 11, p. 17).

1891–92

LCT, with Samuel Colman (1832–1920), decorates the Louisine and Henry O. Havemeyer house at 1 East Sixty-sixth Street and designs his first table lamps.

1892

FEBRUARY 18 Firm is renamed Tiffany Glass and Decorating Company (TGDCo, 1892–1900), located at 333–341 Fourth Avenue.

Driscoll returns to the firm after the death of her husband on February 21.

Lead Glaziers and Glass Cutters Union strikes, demanding reduction of working hours and increase in wages.

LCT forms Women's Glass Cutting Department.

LCT opens a separate glass manufacturing firm under Arthur J. Nash (1849–1934), Stourbridge Glass Company (later Tiffany Furnaces), at Forty-third Avenue and Ninety-seventh Place in Corona, Queens, to manufacture flat glass and blown vessels.

1893

MAY–OCTOBER TGDCo exhibits products at the World's Columbian Exposition in Chicago, including windows and mosaics made by women employees; firm awarded fifty-four medals.

1894

JULY TGDCo exhibits fuel lamps with blown glass shades at its showrooms.

NOVEMBER 13 LCT registers his "Favrile" glass trademark with U.S. Patent Office.

OCTOBER Thirty-five women are working under Driscoll's direction in the Women's Glass Cutting Department, according to Polly King in "Women Workers in Glass at the Tiffany Studios," *Art Interchange* magazine (fig. 4, p. 12).

1895

DECEMBER 26 Siegfried Bing's Paris gallery, L'Art Nouveau, displays a blown glass fuel lamp by TGDCo.

1897

LCT opens foundry and metal workshops in Corona, Queens.

1898

TGDCo publishes a brochure of blown glass fuel lamps, *Tiffany Favrile Glass-Lamps.*

LCT exhibits his first electric lamp at the Salon de la Société Nationale des Beaux-Arts in Paris.

JUNE 15 Driscoll provides her earliest description of a lamp design (*Butterfly*) with a leaded shade in a letter to her family.

JULY She works on a model of the *Dragonfly* lamp.

DECEMBER 5 She reports that her *Daffodil* leaded shade is for sale in Tiffany's showroom.

1899

MAY 2 LCT receives a patent for design of the *Nautilus* lamp.

He exhibits twenty-seven fuel and electric lamps at Grafton Galleries in London, including the *Pond Lily* and Driscoll's *Dragonfly*.

TGDCo publishes an illustrated catalogue, *Lamps and Fixtures*, listing many floral leaded shades.

1900

APRIL–NOVEMBER TGDCo exhibits lamps, Favrile glass, windows, mosaics, and enamels at the Exposition Universelle in Paris; Driscoll's *Dragonfly* lamp wins a bronze medal.

ca. 1901

Driscoll designs the *Wisteria* lamp; fifteen examples are sold by February 1902.

1902

FEBRUARY 25 TGDCo reorganizes as Tiffany Studios (1902–1932).

APRIL–NOVEMBER Tiffany Studios exhibits electric lamps, including the *Wisteria* and *Lily*, at the Turin International Exposition.

1903

APRIL LCT begins construction of Laurelton Hall, his lavish country estate in Oyster Bay, New York, which will include a vast landscape of trees, shrubs, and flowers, such as daffodils, tulips, wisteria, roses, and pond lilies.

Electric models begin to dominate Tiffany Studios' lamp production.

The male-only Lead Glaziers and Glass Cutters Union threatens strike to protest the Women's Glass Cutting Department's work on leaded windows. Agreement between Tiffany Studios and the union limits women's department to twenty-seven workers.

1904

Tiffany Studios publishes *Bronze Lamps*, illustrating twenty-five fuel and electric models, including the *Cobweb*, *Wisteria*, *Peony*, *Poppy*, *Arrowhead*, and *Pagoda*.

APRIL 17 Driscoll's "prize Dragonfly lamp" is mentioned in *New York Daily News*.

OCTOBER Driscoll designs fourteen-inch *Arrowhead*, *Daffodil*, and *Geranium* shades.

1904–05

"Tiffany Girls," flanked by Driscoll and window designer Agnes Northrop (1857–1953), are photographed on the roof of Tiffany Studios at Fourth Avenue and Twenty-fifth Street (fig. 10, p. 16).

1905

OCTOBER Workshops and showrooms move from the Fourth Avenue building to 347 Madison Avenue at Forty-fifth Street.

1906

OCTOBER 1 Tiffany Studios publishes its first *Price List* detailing hundreds of lamps, bases, and shades.

1907

JULY–SEPTEMBER LCT and Driscoll go on a sketching trip to France with Northrop and glass chemist Parker C. McIlhiney (1870–1923).

1909

SEPTEMBER 1 Driscoll marries Edward A. Booth and leaves Tiffany Studios.

1910

OCTOBER 1 Tiffany Studios publishes second *Price List*, indicating discontinuation of most lamp models, including the *Wisteria*, *Trumpet Creeper*, *Apple Blossom*, and *Grape*.

1911

APRIL 15 LCT publishes "The Tasteful Use of Light: Color in Artificial Illumination" in *Scientific American*.

1913

OCTOBER 1 Third *Price List* signals further reduction in lamp production.

OCTOBER 14 Tiffany production manager Leslie H. Nash (1884–1958), a son of Arthur Nash, receives a patent for a "Favrile Fabrique" or "linenfold" shade design, in which glass panels imitate pleated silk.

1915

Tiffany Studios publishes *Tiffany Bronze Lamps*, which illustrates and gives prices for fifty-five models.

1917

MAY–JULY Tiffany Studios sells its building at 347 Madison Avenue and moves operations to smaller quarters at 361 Madison Avenue.

1919

LCT retires.

1920

JANUARY 6 Tiffany Furnaces is reorganized as Louis C. Tiffany Furnaces under the direction of A. Douglas Nash (1881–1940), a son of Arthur Nash.

1924

APRIL 2 Louis C. Tiffany Furnaces is dissolved. Leaded shade production ceases, but sale of unsold stock continues.

1932

APRIL 16 Tiffany Studios files for bankruptcy.

1933

JANUARY 17 LCT dies in New York City.

1944

NOVEMBER 6 Driscoll dies in Ormond Beach, Florida.

RECOMMENDED FOR ADDITIONAL READING

The Charles Hosmer Morse Museum of American Art. "The Louis Comfort Tiffany Chronology." http://www.morsemuseum.org/chronology.

Eidelberg, Martin, Alice Cooney Frelinghuysen, Nancy A. McClelland, and Lars Rachen. *The Lamps of Louis Comfort Tiffany*. New York: Vendome Press, 2005.

Eidelberg, Martin, Nina Gray, and Margaret K. Hofer. *A New Light on Tiffany: Clara Driscoll and the Tiffany Girls*. Exh. cat. New York: New-York Historical Society in association with D Giles Limited, London, 2007.

Frelinghuysen, Alice Cooney. *Louis Comfort Tiffany and Laurelton Hall: An Artist's Country Estate*. Exh. cat. New York: Metropolitan Museum of Art, 2006.

Gray, Nina. *Tiffany by Design: An In-Depth Look at Tiffany Lamps*. Atglen, PA: Schiffer Publishing, 2006.

NOTES

1 Tiffany Studios, *Character and Individuality in Decorations and Furnishings* (New York: Tiffany Studios, 1913), n.p.

2 Clara Driscoll to family members, June 15, 1898, Queens Historical Society, Flushing, NY.

3 The Wolcott Round Robin letters are preserved at the Queens Historical Society and in the Kelso House Collection, Special Collections and Archives, Kent State University Libraries, Kent, OH.

4 Martin Eidelberg, Nina Gray, and Margaret K. Hofer, *A New Light on Tiffany: Clara Driscoll and the Tiffany Girls*, exh. cat. (New York: New-York Historical Society in association with D Giles Limited, London, 2007), fig. 16. See page 23 for Driscoll's description of her meeting with Tiffany to review the design of the lamp.

5 Driscoll describes her idea for the *Dragonfly*, and Tiffany's enthusiasm for the design, in her letter of April 6, 1899, Queens Historical Society, Flushing, NY. See ibid., 97.

6 Ibid.

7 Her prize was mentioned in the *New York Daily News* in April 1904. See Eidelberg, Gray, and Hofer, *A New Light on Tiffany*, fig. 3.

8 The 1906 *Price List* is transcribed in an appendix in Robert Koch, *Louis C. Tiffany's Glass—Bronzes—Lamps* (New York: Crown, 1971).

9 Eidelberg, Gray, and Hofer, *A New Light on Tiffany*, 52–58.

10 See, for instance, Martin Eidelberg et al., *The Lamps of Louis Comfort Tiffany* (New York: Vendome Press, 2005), figs. 75–77, 81.

11 Eidelberg, Gray, and Hofer, *A New Light on Tiffany*, 53, 55.

12 Tiffany focused on producing innovative glass that could not be obtained elsewhere, but he also regularly purchased commercial glass from other manufacturers, including the Opalescent Glass Works in Kokomo, IN, and Leo Popper and Sons in New York City. See Nina Gray, "Glass of All Hues and Colors," in *Tiffany Glass: A Passion for Color*, exh. cat., ed. Rosalind M. Pepall (Montreal: Montreal Museum of Fine Arts, 2009), 106–9; Lindsy R. Parrott, "'Unimaginable Splendours of Color': Tiffany's Opalescent Glass," in *Louis C. Tiffany and the Art of Devotion*, exh. cat., ed. Patricia C. Pongracz (New York: Museum of Biblical Art in association with D Giles Limited, London, 2012), 88–111.

13 Eidelberg, Gray, and Hofer, *A New Light on Tiffany*, 102–3.

14 Ibid., 119–21.

15 Ibid., 184; see also Alice Cooney Frelinghuysen, "Agnes Northrop: Tiffany Studios' Designer of Floral and Landscape Windows," in *Louis C. Tiffany and the Art of Devotion*, 164–83.

16 Mary Jeroleman's Glass Selectors Ledger, Charles Hosmer Morse Museum of American Art, Winter Park, FL. See also Eidelberg, Gray, and Hofer, *A New Light on Tiffany*, 167.

17 Eidelberg et al., *Lamps of Louis Comfort Tiffany*, 33. A ledger documenting orders between 1921 and 1924 sheds light on the popular models of the early 1920s. Tiffany Studios Lamp Department ledger book, 1921–24, Department of American Art, The Metropolitan Museum of Art, New York.

18 Aline B. Saarinen, "Famous, Derided and Revived," *New York Times*, March 13, 1955.

19 Lindsy R. Parrott, "The Glass Archive of the Neustadt Collection of Tiffany Glass," *Journal of Glass Studies* 51 (2009): 161; Patricia Lynden, "'I Am a Very Stubborn Person': A Visit to Dr. Egon Neustadt," *Connoisseur* 209, no. 840 (February 1982): 112.

20 Dr. Egon Neustadt, *The Lamps of Tiffany* (New York: Fairfield Press, 1970), 5.

Conservation of the lamps was supported in part by an award from the National Endowment for the Arts. New-York Historical Society also gratefully acknowledges current and future participants in our Adopt-a-Lamp program.

First published in the United States of America in 2016 by

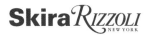

Skira Rizzoli Publications, Inc.
300 Park Avenue South
New York, NY 10010
www.rizzoliusa.com

NEW-YORK
HISTORICAL
SOCIETY
MUSEUM & LIBRARY

2016 2017 2018 2019 / 10 9 8 7 6 5 4 3 2 1

Distributed in the U.S. trade by Random House, New York
Printed in China
ISBN-13: 978-0-8478-4941-3
Library of Congress Catalog Control Number: 2016939613

Designer: Sarah Gifford
Associate Publisher, Skira Rizzoli: Margaret Rennolds Chace
Senior Editor, Skira Rizzoli: Christopher Steighner
Editor, New-York Historical Society: Anne H. Hoy

PAGE 2
Detail of lamp 59

PAGE 4
Detail of lamp 72

ENDPAPERS
Tiffany Studios archival photograph of poppies, ca. 1900. Former collection of Agnes Northrop. Courtesy of Damien Peduto

CREDITS

FIG. 2 Courtesy of Linda D. Alexander; digital retouching, Dick Pratt

FIG. 3 Image © The Metropolitan Museum of Art; image source: Art Resource, NY

FIG. 4 Courtesy of the Ellman Family

FIG. 9 Courtesy of the Ellman Family

FIG. 10 © The Charles Hosmer Morse Foundation, Inc.

FIG. 13 Courtesy of the Neustadt Collection of Tiffany Glass, Queens, NY

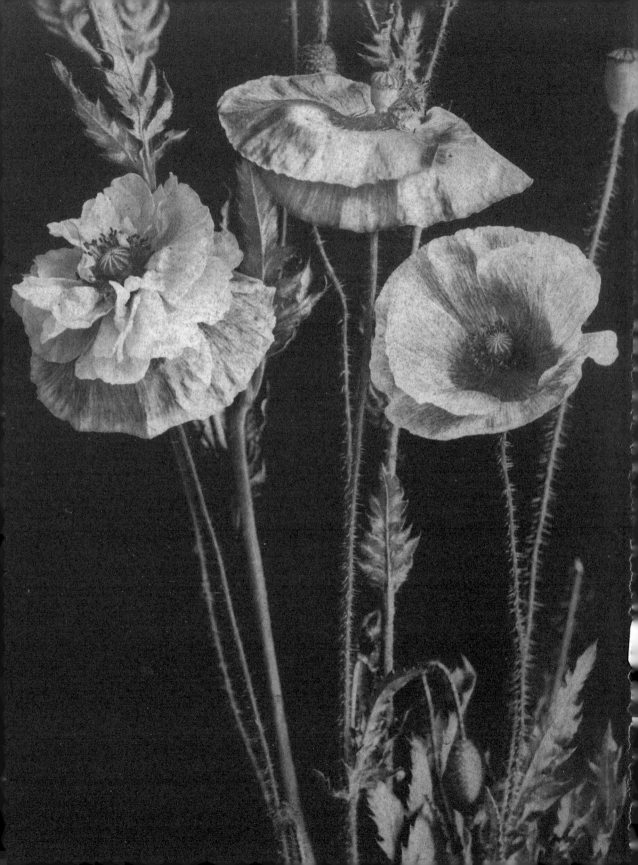